THE TELEBOOK

Chris Kelly

Oxford University Press

Oxford Toronto Melbourne

In Television, things are changing all the time; people and programmes, even whole companies, come and go.

The pace is fast.

Publishing is different. From the start of writing a book to its appearance in the shops can take years. So a book about Television, like this, runs the risk of featuring one or two programmes that may have been axed or rested

But the way those shows are made, the fascinating problems they pose and the questio we need to ask about them do not change.

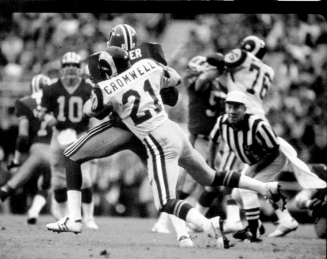

Contents

Lights sprout from the studio ceiling.

Only the audience is in darkness. The conductor stands ready to strike up the band. Performers, cameras and sound are keyed up.

There are seconds to go.

Up in the control room, high above the studio, the director, his production assistant, and vision mixer hope for the best.

The rehearsals have gone well.

Now the efforts of the whole team are about to be seen by millions. No time left for changes. All eyes on the clock.

The countdown begins.
Five, four, three, two, one . . . ON AIR

The young performer

Fire and razzle dazzle

Bonnie Langford

The focus of all the studio activity we saw on the previous page is on the performer. We can best understand how it feels to appear in front of the cameras by looking through the eyes of a young but highly experienced professional.

On stage, in the television studio, and on film Bonnie Langford has established herself as one of the most versatile artists in Britain. She made her first television appearance at the age of six in a programme for new talent. At seven, she was cast in the musical version of *Gone With the Wind* at the Theatre Royal, Drury Lane. By the time she reached the great age of eight, she was a full member of the show business trade union, Equity. Still barely taller than her suitcase, she travelled to America and South Africa with the musical, *Gypsy*, and starred in the film *Bugsy Malone*.

The *Just William* series, in which Bonnie played the appalling Violet Elizabeth, marked a turning point. Following its success, she was offered a number of similar parts but she recognized the danger of type-casting and stood back for a while. Soon her dancing career took off, in tandem with acting, on both stage and television. Her energy, precision, and obvious relish for the work have since won her roles in West End hits (including *Cats* and *The Pirates of Penzance*) and televised spectaculars.

Bonnie soon scotches the notion that the job is glamorous. Although the finished product looks glossy on the screen, there are no frills in the preparation.

Rehearsals

After an initial read-through, rehearsals begin. Typically, Bonnie says, these are held in draughty halls where the heating system has broken down and the parquet floors are spiked with splinters. The canvas backs and seats of the metal-framed chairs have been ripped from their moorings, and the old kettle in the adjoining kitchen has long since refused to boil. The cast fuel themselves with packets of biscuits, until lunchtime in the local pub.

The purpose of these comfortless sessions is to get the actors and dancers thoroughly used to their moves. Failure to hit the exact mark in television, even by as little as a few inches, can easily ruin an entire shot.

The duration of outside rehearsals will vary according to the complexity of the show and the time available. They will be followed by a shorter period of studio rehearsals, using the actual scenery (the 'set') for the production. Finally, the programme will be recorded or, much more rarely, transmitted live.

Facing the camera

Like any other actor or dancer, Bonnie Langford has had to learn that performing for television calls for a quite different technique from performing in the theatre. On stage it is possible to gauge what pleases an

audience by its instant reaction. On television, obviously, the viewers are invisible; if there is a studio audience it will see not just the sequences destined to appear in the completed programme, but also the mistakes, the re-takes, and the long delays. There is not the same feeling of expectancy and excitement as there is behind closed curtains; no dimming of the lights or sounds of tuning up from the orchestra pit.

Facing the cameras without these aids, Bonnie sharpens her concentration by reminding herself that this is a performance which will be seen by millions rather than hundreds; it cannot be improved over

a long run; it has to be right the moment the floor manager gives the cue; and it has to go on being right, take after take, until the director is satisfied.

Then there is the matter of the 'front'. In a theatre there is clearly only one direction in which to aim your performance – towards the paying customers. In television drama you must try not to be aware of the front at all because you are attempting to convey the impression of reality, and in real life we talk to each other rather than to a camera or a row of seats.

But dancers on television inhabit a topsy-turvy world. No sooner have

they established where the front is than a camera angle is altered and they must abruptly point their routine elsewhere. They must also be able to turn from one camera to another, perhaps positioned behind them, and instantly 'spot' it (look it in the eye) without seeming to search for it.

Bonnie Langford describes performing for television as 'like cooking a dinner you don't expect to be eaten'. It is remote from the people who will eventually pass judgement on it. Nevertheless, she finds it challenging precisely because it demands immediate and absolute accuracy. 'You must be on the ball all the time,' she says, 'and then any takes they use will show you at your best.'

Costume design and wardrobe

Mary Morris as Queen Elinor

Leonard Rossiter as King John

Artist's sketches and finished costumes for
a production of King John

Ideally a costume designer will start work on a production by joining in discussions about the script with the director, the set designer, and the make-up designer.

Once the people involved have agreed on what they want the production to look like, the costume designer can begin to plan. This entails breaking down the cast into main parts, supporting actors, and extras (for the crowd scenes). Every item worn by each of them, from underwear outwards, must be right for the period in which the action takes place. The problems are multiplied by the fact that there might be several hundred extras in a single episode.

Costumes come from a number of sources. The BBC, which has by far the largest television wardrobe department in the world, keeps 65,000 outfits in store. Rather forlorn, they hang on racks in warehouses, waiting for their moment of glory.

Eventually the Corporation aims to supply more of its own needs. Meanwhile it frequently has to hire from leading costumiers.

If the production is set in the present, clothes may be bought new from department stores and then made to appear used; this is done by fraying collars and cuffs and stretching trousers until they sag at the knees and seat. The television camera produces such a sharp image that no detail can be overlooked.

Most exciting of all for the costume designer, of course, are the items which have to be created from scratch, especially if they are to represent an age when fashions were elegant. The designer starts with research in books and pictures, and then ideas begin to take shape on the drawing board. Many sketches later, the blueprints will emerge from which tailors and dressmakers can piece together the finished articles. In the case of the BBC, ninety-five per cent of these made-to-measure costumes are entrusted to self-employed 'outworkers' – specialists who prefer to do their work from home.

Whether they come from costumiers, shops, outworkers, or from stock, all costumes have to be assembled with great thoroughness prior to shooting. Wardrobe staff hang them on racks in line-up areas in strict order of wearing. The system means that dressers (who are literally responsible for dressing the cast) can collect the outfits exactly as they are needed for any given scene and deliver them to dressing rooms.

Some actors tend to have their favourites among the hundred or so dressers employed by the BBC and ask their advice on everything from lacing up whalebone corsets to the approved way of holding a fan.

As well as supervising the making of some costumes and the coming and going of thousands more (remember that in a large company there will be several drama productions in progress at any one time), wardrobe departments also keep a reserve of accessories. BBC stockrooms bulge with enough hats, feather boas, ties, collars, cufflinks, shoes, umbrellas, and the like to supply the jumble sales of Britain for a decade.

Large-scale series obviously offer costume designers their greatest challenge and satisfaction, but designing for light entertainment can be rewarding too. A twelve-week showcase for a glamorous star will call for the creation of original, stylish, expensive dresses which will not merely set the tone for the programmes but may also advance a career.

From creatures great to creatures small, the clothes worn by the dolls in Playschool did not simply happen; they too are the work of costume designers.

Job spot
If you think you have a feel for costume, it is important to decide where your interest really lies; is it in making or designing? It is rare for dressmakers to become designers. The BBC likes its costume designers and design assistants to have a degree in either theatre design or fashion design, while those who prefer to make costumes should have completed a dressmaking course.

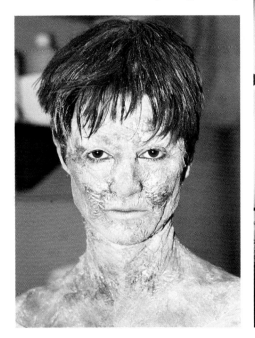

Janet Fielding being made up

Make-up

Putting on a new face

The main aim of a make-up artist is to achieve a natural look, almost as though nothing artificial has been applied at all. If an actress or a news-reader on television looks too obviously made-up, then the job has been done badly.

There is no problem when presenters appear as themselves. All they need is a powder base to take away the shine from the face. The real challenge is a 'character' make-up, especially one which involves ageing. The process may take several hours.

Pads are glued under the eyes with a spirit-gum to make them puffy. The skin is then stretched, while a rubber solution is applied with a stippling sponge. As it dries, the flesh wrinkles.

The make-up artist then applies shading and highlighting. Finally, the face can be crowned with a wig (the best are made of human hair) and finished off with added touches like nicotine-stained teeth, or even custom-made dentures.

A make-up artist carries the tools of the trade in a large box. It contains everything that could possibly be useful in any situation. As well as the basic items – a mirror, sable brushes, scissors, a hairdrier, rollers, combs, tissues, etc. – there are palettes with shades blended to the artist's own preference: glycerine for tears, artificial blood called Kensington Gore (for a 'congealed' wound this is sometimes mixed with bran or even Rice Krispies), eye-shadow, hair-whitener, glitter dust, and galleries of plastic bottles full of cleansing spirits.

As well as being creative, a make-up artist must be something of an amateur psychologist. Actors sitting in the chair are at their most nervous and vulnerable. Since the make-up department is their last stop before going on to the studio floor, it is vital to make them feel confident and relaxed.

How to get in

This combination of tact and technique accounts for the fact that television make-up training may take four years or more. Competition for vacancies is fierce. One major company annually advertises two jobs on average and gets two hundred applications. Requirements vary, but this same company only interviews hopefuls who are twenty-one or over, have A-level passes in Art, History and English, and have done courses in hairdressing and beauty therapy.

Job spot

For the lucky ones who get in, days are long and the work is hard. It is not unusual, on location, to start at seven in the morning and finish at nine in the evening. And the surroundings may be anything but glamorous. On the other hand the rates of pay are good, no two productions are alike, and there is the satisfaction of seeing the results on the screen.

1 The actress before make-up begins.

2 The make-up artist discusses the make-up with the actress.

3 Latex solution is applied with a stippling sponge. Cotton-wool pads are glued under the eyes to make them puffy.

4 The skin is dried with a hair-dryer.

6 Teeth stain is applied.

5 The latex has now wrinkled the skin.

SET DESIGN

Creating heaven and earth

'I went out and said: "Can I have that meadow please?' It sounds more like God than a mere mortal but that was how Roy Stonehouse, prize-winning Head of Design at Granada, stunned the company's Props Department when he was working on *King Lear*. It proved to be one of the most extraordinary productions ever seen on British television.

In order to spare Lord Olivier the strain of prolonged outdoor shooting in the foul weather conditions envisaged by Shakespeare, the entire play was recorded in a large studio over a three and a half week span – hence the mobile meadow. Stonehouse chose his grassy spot in the Cheshire countryside and had it transported piecemeal on a double-level low-loader back to Manchester. There, in Studio 12, the two hundred yards of turf was laid over three thousand sandbags, which in turn rested on a scaffolding framework. The effect was crowned with an oak tree, suitably blackened by lightning, and 3,500 clumps of heather. By the end of the week, after careful watering, the grass had started to grow.

Sharing the studio with the fragrant mound were a running stream, complete with plant life, a copse in which butterflies fluttered, a beach, and a hovel made of real logs. Meanwhile the floor-space had been lined with plastic, and the lighting-grid hung with rain-bars ready for a three-day indoor downpour, during which 900 gallons of water fell from the studio sky. To protect the many electrical outlets round the walls, the longest shower curtain in the world was improvised – 230 feet by 39-feet high.

On Friday night, after five days of shooting, the bilge pumps worked overtime to drain the floor ready for the setting in of two palaces and a courtyard by Monday morning.

Since the period chosen for the action was the year 800, there were few sources the designer could turn to for accurate information, either about the buildings themselves or the furniture inside them. Once again he used heavy logs for the exteriors, spraying them green at the bottom as though the damp had naturally spread upwards from the ground.

Week Three saw the woodwork replaced by a two-thirds size replica of Stonehenge, modelled with 4,500 cubic feet of polystyrene and 5 tons of plaster. That in turn made way for the French and English camps.

The entire design project on *King Lear* was completed by Roy Stonehouse with the help of one assistant. First they discussed the project together and then moved on to photographs, drawings, quarter-inch scale plans detailing elevation and section, and paper models to show how much room there was for manoeuvre. They were responsible for overseeing every stage of costing, buying, construction, painting, and setting in. Their design budget for the production was £140,000. When you consider that the play ran two and a half hours and will stand numerous repeats, the figure is not unreasonable.

Although in studio terms *King Lear* was an unusually ambitious operation, it illustrates the sort of problems a television designer may be expected to solve in the most effective and economical way.

A challenge on that scale is of course a reward for talent and experience. Starting at a more modest level, design embraces every graphic, backing, desk and chair, every setting either real or imagined, indoors and out. For each of them, as for *King Lear*, the principle remains the same: the designer interprets visually what the producer, the director, and the writer have in mind.

Think of an idea

Getting it together

Any television programme or series starts with an idea, and when it comes to ideas there are no rules. It might be a suggestion which has been sitting in a drawer for ages until suddenly the time seems right for it; it may have occurred to someone on the way to work; it could be prompted by a story in a newspaper or a book, by a telephone call or a chance meeting.

Almost any subject, dealt with imaginatively, can form the basis of a programme.

Some of the best ideas seem at first sight the most ordinary. Who would have thought, for instance, that you could make a gripping natural history half-hour about the inhabitants of a compost heap or a long-running series about life in a drab Northern street?

Most shows spring from the minds of the people who make them. That is what they are paid for. But there is nothing to stop you offering *your* thoughts. As we will see, *Blue Peter* actually invites viewers to do just that. At the end of the book you will find the address of every television company in Britain. It has to be said that they are all bombarded with suggestions, most of which are unsuitable. They might be too boring,

too expensive, or they may simply have been done before. But yours could still be a winner. Explain it on one side of a sheet of paper (most television producers have neither the time nor the patience to read more) set it out clearly and neatly, and send it off. If you want to submit a script, you can see how to present it elsewhere in the book. Finally, always be sure to keep a copy yourself; television people are good at losing things.

Different departments work in slightly different ways. Since we have been dealing with acting, make-up, costume and production design, we will concentrate on drama.

The producer

Once an idea has been accepted and before a big, costly production can begin, approval has to be given by the

head of a company (usually the managing director) and the head of programmes (programme controller). That leaves the ball with the department head (in this case the head of drama), who will either mastermind the project personally or give it to a producer.

At this stage the leading figures involved will know roughly how much they need to spend (the budget). The next step is to commission a writer who will be told exactly what is wanted. Provided that the producer is happy with it, the delivery of the script is the signal for the team to grow much larger.

The director – and his army
Words and money are useless without pictures, so the producer must appoint a director and a designer.

Together the producer and director, working closely with the casting director and the contracts department, will choose the actors they want for the piece.

An army of colleagues, with special skills, from other departments is called in. Depending on the size and style of the drama, they will include all, or most, of the following: production assistant, production manager, script editor, cameramen and women (studio, film and/or Outside Broadcast), sound, lighting, floor managers, accounts, secretaries, wardrobe, make-up, researchers, librarians (film, music and reference books), set dressers, carpenters, props, stills photographers, painters, stage crew, callboys or girls, riggers, drivers, firemen, stuntmen, location caterers, and possibly union shop

stewards in case of disputes. The studio sequences will also call for a vision mixer, a technical supervisor, VTR, and telecine.

When shooting is over, more experts swell the numbers: a composer and musicians, processing laboratories, editors of film, tape, and sound, and a dubbing mixer.

Launching the finished article may bring in sales, publicity, and public relations. And, as we shall discover, seeing the play off the premises and on its way to our television set is the job of the transmission controller.

Organizations may differ in detail but there are no short cuts. Each bit of the jigsaw is essential. So when your idea for a major drama series is accepted, bear in mind the pyramid of people it takes to bring it to the screen.

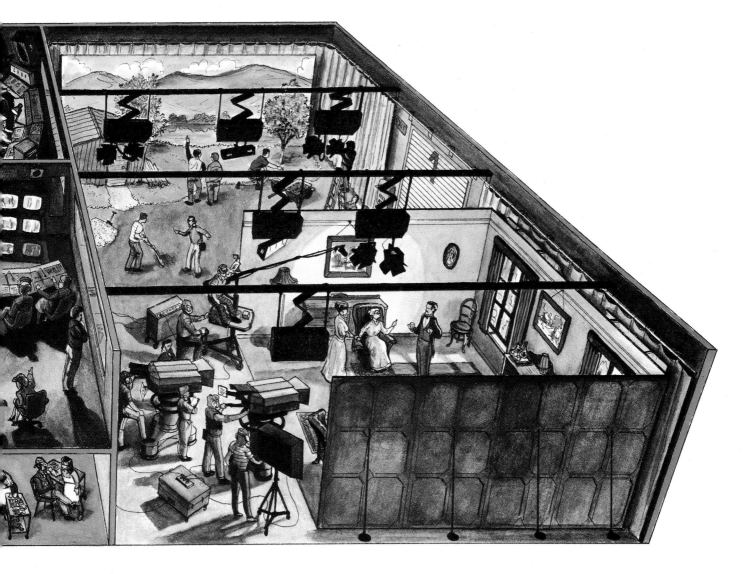

The networks

When Dr Samuel Johnson published his great *Dictionary of the English Language* in 1755, 'network' was one of the words that he found hardest to define. According to him it meant: 'any thing reticulated or decussated at equal distances, with interstices between the intersections.' Most readers must have looked up from the book more baffled than when they opened it.

Nowadays, when we talk of a network, we are likely to be discussing broadcasting. Programmes which are 'networked' are those which are seen by a national (as distinct from a local or regional) audience. But just to confuse matters, some ITV shows are partially networked; that is to say they are transmitted in a number of areas, though not nationwide.

The older of the television networks, the BBC, can be thought of as a pyramid. At the top are the London studios and offices with their headquarters at the Television Centre, Shepherds Bush. Here the chief concern is to make or to buy programmes for a national audience (and to sell some abroad).

In the middle of the pyramid are the six network production centres in the provinces: Birmingham, Manchester, Bristol, Cardiff, Glasgow and Belfast. Their job is to serve their own areas, to produce some material for the country as a whole and, if necessary, to provide facilities for productions masterminded from London. By specializing, these centres have contributed greatly to the overall strength of the Corporation. Bristol, for instance, has cornered the market in wildlife programmes and Birmingham has a good reputation for drama.

At the base of the BBC television structure are the so-called 'island sites': Norwich, Nottingham, Newcastle, Leeds, Plymouth, Southampton, Edinburgh, Aberdeen, Dundee, Bangor, and Swansea. From time to time work from these will be viewed nationally, but they are chiefly designed to offer a local service. (Presumably that is why they are known as 'island sites' – because, except in news terms, they have less urgent links with 'mainland' London.)

The rival network, ITV, consists of fifteen individual companies, each owned by shareholders. Between them, the fifteen companies fund ITN and Channel Four. The 'majors' (Thames, London Weekend, Central, Granada, Yorkshire) and the regional companies (Grampian, Scottish, Tyne Tees, Border, Ulster, Anglia, TV South, Television South West, Channel, HTV) were all selected and appointed by the Independent Broadcasting Authority, as was the early morning station, TV-am. After a period of years, fixed by Parliament, the IBA examines the record of each company and decides whether or not it deserves to have its contract renewed.

Meanwhile the IBA also supervises programme planning, controls advertising on ITV and owns the transmitters.

In a typical ITV area, about half the programming screened in a given week will have been made by the five majors. The other half comprises material made by the ten regional companies and judged suitable for a national showing: purely local programmes from the station serving the area; news from ITN; and shows which come from outside ITV (for example American series).

Top left: Central's new studio complex in Nottingham
Above: Anglia Television's headquarters in Norwich
Left: BBC Television Centre at Wood Lane in London

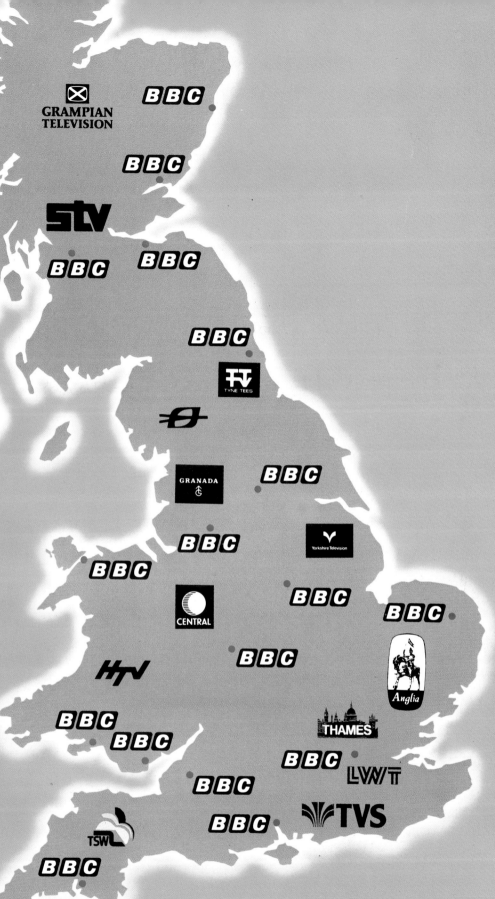

Britain's most famous street

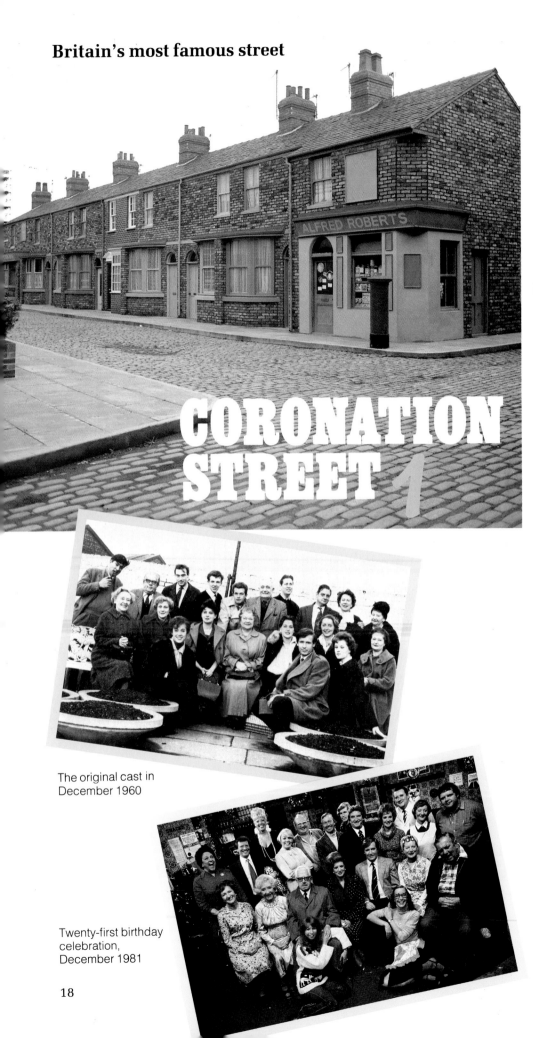

CORONATION STREET 1

The original cast in December 1960

Twenty-first birthday celebration, December 1981

Behind the facade of the Street

Tony Warren, who worked in the Granada Promotions Department in Manchester came up with the idea for the series in the summer of 1960. He wanted to call it *Florizel Street* but the title was rejected because it sounded too much like a disinfectant. *Jubilee Street* was a front-runner for a while but finally the first producer opted for *Coronation Street*.

The aim was simply to mirror life in a Northern working class neighbourhood where, Warren claimed, the underlying forces were 'a fascinating freemasonry' and 'a volume of unwritten rules'.

The programme made its debut on 9 December 1960. In those days one of the two weekly episodes was transmitted live – a nerve-racking experience both for the actors and the production team. Within a short time it built up an enormous following and it has been among the most popular shows on the network ever since, often topping the ratings.

Coronation Street owes its success to the fact that, with the honourable exception of EastEnders, it has consistently been better written, acted, and produced than any other British soap opera. Some of its regulars have deservedly become part of the national folklore.

One of the most important figures behind the scenes is the programme's historian. His job is to keep an up-to-date index of all the characters, past and present, with a note of what they did in each episode, details of their children, friends and relations – even a reminder of their favourite drink so that the writers will know what they would order in the Rover's Return.

A background was also invented for the Street itself. Its imaginary history began in 1896 when it was built to house the workers from Charles Hardcastle's cotton mill. The name coined for the area as a whole was Weatherfield.

Most of the action takes place in the Rover's, the corner shop, and the living rooms of the leading characters. These interior scenes are recorded in the studio. When the script calls for dialogue outside in the Street, cast and cameras move to an exterior set, completely redeveloped in 1982. To make it look authentic, 49,000 old bricks and 6,500 slates were reclaimed from local demolition sites, and the mortar was blackened with ash. Viewers had noticed that in the original set there was no gap between the Rover's and Albert Tatlock's house. Since the pub had an outside gents' lavatory, this meant that

customers going out of the front door in search of it must have ended up in Albert's parlour. Under the circumstances it was hardly surprising that he always looked disgruntled. Sure enough in the new set a narrow alleyway divides the two buildings.

Visitors to the location, who have included the Queen and Prince Philip, could be forgiven for believing that they are in a real road inhabited by real people. No detail has been

overlooked. But open one of the doors and the illusion is instantly destroyed. The houses are just shells lined with breeze-blocks. Only the Rover's is partially furnished so that the cast can relax during breaks in shooting.

Because the settings are outwardly convincing and the figures in them believable, some members of the public are inclined to confuse fiction with fact. Whenever a house in the Street becomes vacant through the storyline, there are letters from viewers eager to rent it. Characters with problems attract scores of sympathetic suggestions, and at Christmas groups regularly write to ask if they can hold their staff party at the Rover's.

Rover's Return: a pub with no beer

The most famous pub in the world sells no beer; in fact it sells nothing at all. Characters who order a pint of bitter brewed by the mythical brewery, Newton and Ridley's, get a bottled shandy which has been poured into a pressurized barrel and pulled through a pump. Vimto doubles for rum and for red wine; white wine and gin consist of

lime juice mixed with water. The drink to avoid is whisky – the recipe used by the props department for that is a cocktail of lime juice and gravy browning.

The Rover's Return is the heart of Coronation Street. It is the focal point, the social centre, where all the characters meet on an equal footing. In the Rover's, individual stories become the business of the whole community and take on a greater dramatic significance.

Over the years the building itself has suffered as great a buffeting as any of its customers. Scarcely had it recovered from the floods of 1975 when a runaway lorry rearranged the brickwork. It has even been the site of buried treasure. In one episode twenty gold sovereigns, hidden by a former landlord, were discovered in the cellar.

CORONATION STREET 2

Planning a twice-weekly serial is a complex and demanding operation. In a sense, *Coronation Street* is television by numbers.

The story
Every third Monday the producer calls a story conference to which are summoned the writers (on average there are nine working on the programme), the two storyline writers, and the historian. The object of the meeting is to hammer out ideas for six episodes which will be shown over a three week period in roughly three months' time.

Guided by the conference, the storyline writers will provide detailed outlines of all the six episodes, breaking them down into separate scenes and explaining exactly what happens, to whom and why. Even the minor characters, on the fringe of the action, will be taken into account.

On the Monday morning of the third week the producer commissions a writer for each of the six shows, handing out the suggested storylines. If the writers are not happy with them, they have a chance to say so at yet another conference when ideas are finalized. They then have two weeks in which to complete their script.

The production schedule
The production schedule also works to a pattern of threes, which at this stage begins to sound like a nightmarish question in a maths exam.

Three directors work on the programme at any one time, each on a three-week cycle or 'turn-round'. While Director A collects two fresh scripts, Director B, having already done so, will now be in the second week of preparation, and Director C will be in his or her third week – the final phase of rehearsal and recording.

Week 1
For all directors the process starts with a series of meetings. Should the scripts call for new sets, the designer

will be consulted. Shooting on location will involve an Outside Broadcast Unit or the Film Department. A storyline may introduce previously unseen characters, in which case the casting department will recommend actors.

Week 2

The director's next step is to prepare camera scripts – precise plans of the way in which the episodes will be visualized, telling each story with perhaps two hundred shots shared between three cameras. These instructions are typed and distributed by the production assistant.

Week 3

The last week begins with any exterior shooting which may be necessary. There follow two days of rehearsals leading up to a Technical Run on the Wednesday afternoon. This is a chance for the lighting director, the technical supervisor, the senior cameraman and the sound supervisor to see if the action poses any special problems. The producer will also be able to assess performances, while the production assistant does an accurate timing. Over-runs are easily dealt with by cutting dialogue. Under-runs can mean lengthening or even adding scenes.

By three o'clock on Thursday afternoon all the indoor sets have been erected in the studio, the props are in place, the lighting director has positioned the lights to get the best out of each sequence, Cameras and Sound know their moves. During the next day and a half, until six-thirty on Friday evening, the director rehearses and records both episodes, scene by scene, not necessarily sticking to the order in which they appear in the script.

After the weekend the director edits the programmes and collects scripts for two more, setting off on a fresh cycle. Transmission in Britain of the finished shows will be in three weeks. It may be months or even years before audiences see them abroad, in the many countries where *Coronation Street* is sold.

CORONATION STREET *The script*

Camera Script

These two pages of script, reproduced by kind permission of the author, Peter Whalley, and Granada Television Ltd, are part of an episode of Coronation Street screened at the end of December 1983.

If you send a script to a television company, you should set it out like this – with the exception of the instructions to the cameramen down the left hand side. You will find a key to those below.

The conversation is between the owner of the corner shop, Alf Roberts and Rita Fairclough. Her husband, Len, has just been killed in a car crash. She is convinced that on the night he died, he called on another woman. Alf is trying to reassure her. Sharon, whom we meet very briefly, is the foster child of Rita and the late Len.

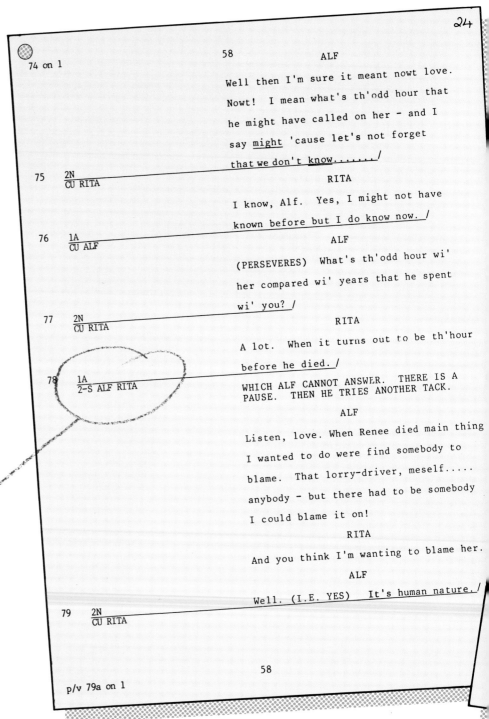

```
 74 on 1            58              ALF

                         Well then I'm sure it meant nowt love.
                         Nowt!  I mean what's th'odd hour that
                         he might have called on her - and I
                         say might 'cause let's not forget
                         that we don't know......../

 75    2N                              RITA
       CU RITA
                         I know, Alf.  Yes, I might not have
                         known before but I do know now. /

 76    1A                              ALF
       CU ALF
                         (PERSEVERES)  What's th'odd hour wi'
                         her compared wi' years that he spent
                         wi' you? /

 77    2N                              RITA
       CU RITA
                         A lot.  When it turns out to be th'hour
                         before he died. /

 78    1A                WHICH ALF CANNOT ANSWER.  THERE IS A
       2-S ALF RITA      PAUSE.  THEN HE TRIES ANOTHER TACK.

                                       ALF

                         Listen, love. When Renee died main thing
                         I wanted to do were find somebody to
                         blame.  That lorry-driver, meself.....
                         anybody - but there had to be somebody
                         I could blame it on!

                                       RITA

                         And you think I'm wanting to blame her.

                                       ALF

                         Well. (I.E. YES)   It's human nature. /

 79    2N
       CU RITA



                                 58

 p/v 79a on 1
```

Key to camera instructions

The figures at the extreme left hand side of the script are the shots into which the dialogue is divided. Reading across, the next number is the camera taking the shot and the adjacent letter is the position occupied by that camera on the studio plan drawn up by the director. **CU** stands for close-up. So, to use the example of shot 75; it will be a close-up of Rita, taken by camera two in position N.

2-S: two-shot; a shot which includes two people.

p/v: preview. 'p/v 79a on 1' at the bottom of page 58 is a reminder that the next shot will be 79a on camera one. Before cutting to it, the director can pre-view it on one of the monitor screens in the control room.

OOV: out of vision; the character is heard but not yet seen.

MS: mid-shot, usually from head to waist. So on shot 80, camera three in position J starts with a mid-shot of Sharon as she comes in and then widens (loosens) to include Alf and Rita in a three-shot.

Q: short form of Cue; an instruction by sound or signal to a performer or an engineer. **'Q Bell'** on page 59 of the

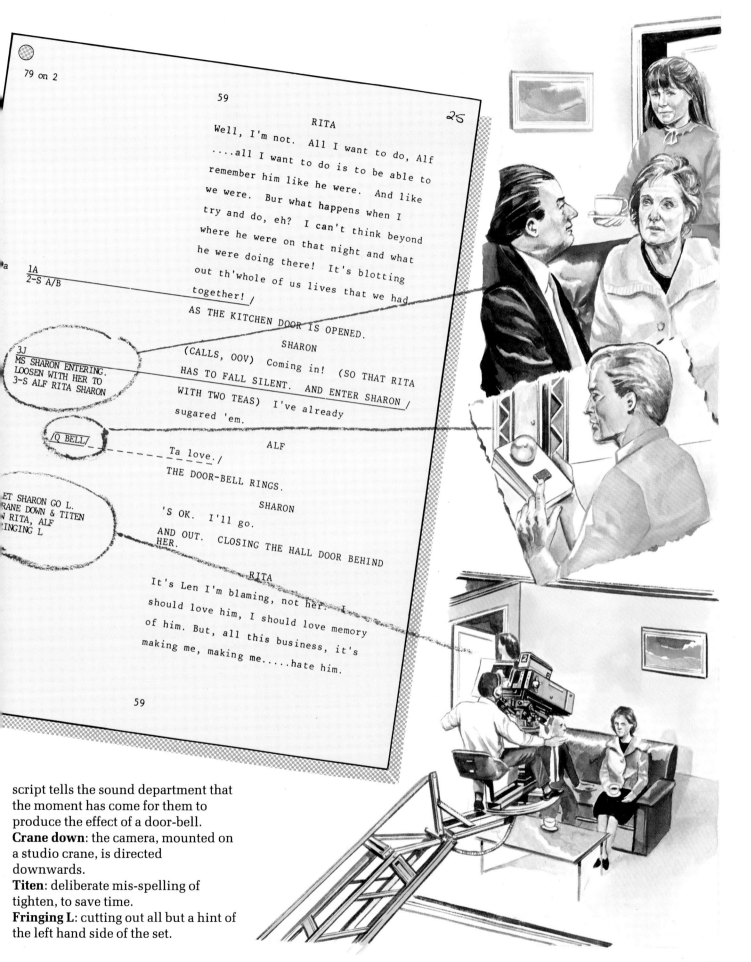

59

RITA

Well, I'm not. All I want to do, Alf
....all I want to do is to be able to
remember him like he were. And like
we were. Bur what happens when I
try and do, eh? I can't think beyond
where he were on that night and what
he were doing there! It's blotting
out th'whole of us lives that we had
together! /

AS THE KITCHEN DOOR IS OPENED.

SHARON

(CALLS, OOV) Coming in! (SO THAT RITA
HAS TO FALL SILENT. AND ENTER SHARON
WITH TWO TEAS) I've already
sugared 'em.

ALF

Ta love. /

THE DOOR-BELL RINGS.

SHARON

'S OK. I'll go.
AND OUT. CLOSING THE HALL DOOR BEHIND
HER.

RITA

It's Len I'm blaming, not her. I
should love him, I should love memory
of him. But, all this business, it's
making me, making me.....hate him.

59

1A
2-S A/B

3J
MS SHARON ENTERING.
LOOSEN WITH HER TO
3-S ALF RITA SHARON

/Q BELL/

ET SHARON GO L.
RANE DOWN & TITEN
N RITA, ALF
INGING L

25

script tells the sound department that
the moment has come for them to
produce the effect of a door-bell.

Crane down: the camera, mounted on
a studio crane, is directed
downwards.

Titen: deliberate mis-spelling of
tighten, to save time.

Fringing L: cutting out all but a hint of
the left hand side of the set.

Commercial Break 1

Selling on television

Television commercials are the best way of advertising most products because they are seen by so many people, all at the same time. Whereas a newspaper or a magazine may have a few hundred thousand readers, a top-rating programme could reach more than 16,000,000 viewers. Even if half of them decide to put the kettle on during the commercial break, the message is still getting through to a large part of the population. And the same will be true week after week until the campaign comes to an end.

Advertising agencies

Persuading us to buy is a highly specialized business. It is handled by advertising agencies, some of which operate internationally.

A big company may employ several agencies at once, sometimes using one to check that the others are doing their job efficiently. When millions of pounds are invested in selling a new soap powder, for example, the manufacturers want to be sure that they are getting value for money.

A company may choose the agencies it hires for a variety of reasons: because of their skill at buying space in the press or time on television, for their creative ability, or simply on personal grounds.

Often three or four agencies will be invited to compete for a single account. They will all go to great lengths to win, thinking nothing of spending £50,000 or more on the gamble. They interview members of the public to find out what is likely to appeal to them, come up with what we call ideas but they call concepts, make beautifully illustrated treatments to show how the campaign will look, write sample scripts, recommend ways of using television, and generally try to prove that they are the best.

The winners stand to gain a large sum. For the losers, there is no consolation. There are times when all the contestants are disappointed: the company may decide to use none of them.

Battle tactics

Once a manufacturer has engaged an agency to launch a product, together they will agree on a media plan – in other words, battle tactics. What sort of people is the advertising aimed at? Which is the most effective way of reaching them? Should the campaign start in just one region or should it go nationwide from the beginning? What time would be best for a television commercial? (If the product is a game for children, there is clearly not much point in putting it on the screen late in the evening.)

When answers have been found to all these questions and many more, experts in the agency concerned will literally set about buying time. Each of the fifteen ITV companies has a rate card – a price list – which tells the buyers how much it will cost them to place a commercial in any given break throughout the broadcasting day. It goes without saying that a slot after *Coronation Street*, a series which is regularly watched by the biggest audience of the week, will be much more expensive than thirty seconds after a documentary about basket weaving.

What did the viewers think?

The screening of a commercial is by no means the end of the story. It is obviously vital to gauge whether it is having any impact. One agency does this by limiting the first showing to the commercial break during *News at Ten* in a single ITV region. The following morning a team of researchers is sent to ask viewers if they saw the commercial, what it was about, who was in it, and what they thought of it. Should the results fail to add up to a certain number of points on a fixed scale, the advertisement is withdrawn, changed, and then placed again in the same spot. When it reaches a satisfactory score, it is given a national airing.

Occasionally manufacturers forget that advertising actually works and are unprepared for the sudden demand created by a successful television campaign. In that event, the commercial has to be rested while stocks of the product are rushed to the shops.

What do *you* think?

Some people think that there is too much advertising on television. Do you? Others argue that there should be even more; that the BBC should be allowed to show commercials too, so that it could generate the money it needs without depending on the licence fee, which is fixed by the Government and is never high enough for the liking of programme makers.

It is a good idea to give these things some thought and – if you are unhappy with the service you get – to say so.

DOCTOR WHO

Who needs it?

1 roll 500 mm bandage
28 lbs fast-setting potters' plaster
4 sq yds hessian scrim
½ pint shellac
6 lbs layup resin
1 tub barrier cream
Sink plunger

Can you guess what a class of sixth formers would be making if they went shopping for these strange items? The answer is a Dalek. The complete list of parts and paint runs to a whole page, which is issued by the BBC with instructions for assembly to practical viewers who want a do-it-yourself version of public enemy number one. To make sure that the design works, the Corporation asked the technical sixth formers of Highbury Grove School in London to try it out in their workshop. With the help of teachers, they produced a magnificent replica at a cost of £12. Nowadays, unfortunately, the bill would be considerably higher.

The Daleks made their first appearance in *Dr Who* shortly after the series began in 1963. Twenty years later, when the programme marked the start of its third decade with an Easter celebration at Longleat, the Daleks were still among the most popular attractions. At a charity auction held as part of the same event, a coat worn by the fourth Dr Who, Tom Baker, raised £810.

Who invented Who?

Sidney Newman and Donald Wilson are credited with launching the ageless time-traveller on his epic journeys. In the early nineteen-sixties, they felt that the time was right for a mixture of history and science fiction. Newman and Wilson encouraged producer, Verity Lambert, to aim for an audience of eight to fourteen year-olds. She realized, however, that the idea could also attract adults and she was proved right. It is now estimated that some sixty per cent of the viewers are over sixteen. Many parents who watched Dr Who in their youth enjoy seeing the reaction of their children to the daring eccentric. He has become, in fact, a family doctor.

Who buys Who?

The fame of the *Tardis* (the letters stand for Time And Relative Dimensions In Space) has spread far beyond the British Isles. The inter-galactic meanderings of the wayward space-craft have regularly been seen in fifty countries by an audience of more than a hundred million. Devoted fans in the United States hold conventions to which they often invite the producer of the show.

Worldwide exposure has created a large market for products bearing the Dr Who imprint; they have included Easter eggs, underpants, tea-caddies, tents, money-boxes, pencil-cases, mugs, posters, Dalek bubble-baths, and even rolls of wallpaper. The programme is one of the biggest earners for BBC Enterprises, which is the sales-arm of the Corporation.

Who needs ideas?

In order to keep storylines fresh and original, the producer asks writers to submit ideas. If these look promising, there will then be a request for a scene breakdown, detailing the development of each episode. Finally a script will be commissioned. On one occasion an eighteen year-old, Andrew Smith of Rutherglen, was asked to write for the series after he had patiently bombarded the office with suggestions over a long period.

Who is Who?

The creators of Dr Who came up with a format which allows of infinite variety. Our hero is limited by neither time nor space. In his never-ending fight against evil he can overcome every catastrophe. Along the way he serves us with a concoction of fantasy, whimsical humour, pretend-science, and danger. He can change his companions whenever he becomes bored with them and has himself enjoyed several incarnations. The character is so versatile that it would be no great surprise if, in a future season, Dr Who turned up as a woman.

Although *Dr Who* was rested by the BBC, the series has, in a special way, been shared and enjoyed by two generations.

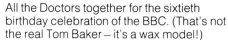

All the Doctors together for the sixtieth birthday celebration of the BBC. (That's not the real Tom Baker – it's a wax model!)

The Endurance

The *Endurance* is held tight in the grip of polar ice; parts of the hull are starting to buckle. Unable to sail any further. Ernest Shackleton and his party of explorers will be forced to camp out on the floes.

On television the dramatic scene looks absolutely real. In fact it is a creation of the BBC Visual Effects department (the BBC prefers to call

Special Effects 'Visual Effects'). The location is Greenland, doubling for the Antarctic, and the ship is a model some twenty five feet long.

The miniature *Endurance* began its epic voyage in London. It was built in sections, of lightweight materials like polystyrene, packed in boxes small enough to fit into the luggage-hold of an aircraft and assembled at its chilly destination. On the last lap, it was hauled by twelve huskies. They hurtled along at such a rate that the production team was unable to keep up.

When shooting was finished, the strange vessel was offered to the local people but it was swept out to sea before they could dismantle it.

From North Acton to the North Pole

SPECIAL **EFFECTS**

For the BBC Visual Effects unit, the largest of its kind in the world, there are no typical assignments; each show poses different problems. Between them, fifty designers and assistants are responsible for the Special Effects in every kind of programme – from documentary to light entertainment, from drama to news. There is even a group attached to the Open University at Milton Keynes, building three-dimensional models of scientific concepts.

What are Special Effects? The head of the BBC unit defines them as 'the recreation of natural phenomena on cue'; in other words, making things which are usually beyond our control happen when and where we want them to. For example, we unfortunately have no say in the timing of earthquakes, but Special Effects experts can produce convincing seismic shocks at the

press of a button. At a simpler level, they can trigger explosions, big or small, precisely when they are called for by the script.

A walk through the BBC Visual Effects workshops at North Acton reveals the range of the projects on hand. A designer has just begun to copy an early printing press: the work

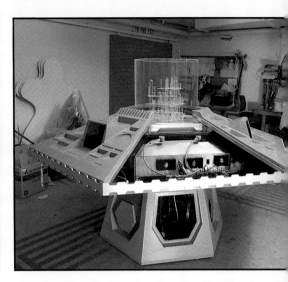

will take a month or more. Rows of rubbery heads and hands, modelled from life, are evidence of historical horrors. The finishing touches are being put to an unnamed planet for BBC Scotland. A British Leyland hen, complete with perspex laying-flap, roosts contentedly after its moment of comic glory. Chunks of ceiling, made of expanded polyurethane and balsa wood, look realistic enough to fool a builder.

Sometimes the effects which we take for granted can be deceptively difficult to achieve. Imagine, for instance, a cosy scene with an open fire. Although the action may only occupy three minutes of screen time, it could take three hours to shoot, during which the fuel and flames must not alter. The solution to that problem is a gas bottle and artificial logs.

Special Effects designers need to be accomplished all-rounders. As well as working closely with directors, they may be called upon to direct model sequences themselves. They must also be capable of producing a snowstorm (using substances which include fire-fighting foam and even Epsom Salts); setting up a stained glass window

which will shatter when a singer hits a high note; making a body, cut down from a gibbet, turn to dust before our eyes; and modelling a perfect reproduction of the Palace of Westminster. Although they may sound fanciful, those are all actual examples of challenges faced by BBC Visual Effects designers. Their ingenuity is on trial every day and the results are watched critically by millions, who are now used to the brilliant effects created at great expense on the cinema screen.

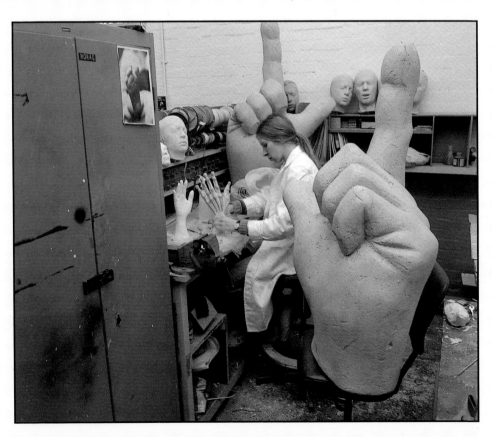

Pills, telephones and weight-lifting

Tomorrow's World

The pace of scientific discovery is rapidly accelerating. Literally every day we learn more about the origins of the universe, the planet on which we live, the diseases which afflict us, ways of producing more and better crops, and the most effective means of communicating with each other. No one can hope to take it all in, but television is particularly good at passing on at least a fraction of that information in words and pictures that we can all understand.

4.15 pm Stagger-through

In the gallery of a smallish studio at the BBC Television Centre, the production team are standing by for the first rehearsal (known as a 'stagger-through') of Tomorrow's World, due to be transmitted live in under three hours time.

Cued by the floor manager, the presenters in the studio do a complete run-through of the programme, getting used to their moves and the props they will have to handle.

Maggie Philbin rehearsing with a gadget to lift heavy weights

Setting up for the item on the radio-telephone system

A disappointing trickle of pills

5.15 pm Editor's meeting

The presenters join the editor in the gallery for a meeting. Among the others present are the producer of the week, the assistant producers (each of whom has researched and compiled one of the six items in the show), the unit manager, director, production assistant, and vision mixer. The number is unusually large because the series devours material at a rapid rate. It is also seen by the BBC as a training ground for potential producers and directors.

The stagger-through has revealed problems. Lights, which should have beamed brightly under a colourful display panel, failed even to glimmer. Pills, which were supposed to gush like a waterfall out of a giant bottle, just dribbled on to the floor. Most

important of all, the production assistant consults her stop-watch and announces that the programme is running two minutes too long. As it happens, the producer is relieved. She feels that the last story is saying 'far too much about far too little'; a cut will improve it. Everyone chips in, to the constant accompaniment of telephone calls, but the last word is left to the editor. As the meeting breaks up, the presenters have twenty minutes in which to do the necessary re-writes, while the director plans new shots.

Presenters and editor sorting out final problems

6.30 pm
Second rehearsal

Things are going more smoothly now. This time the pills tumble out in a torrent. There are no more headaches either with the coloured lights, illuminating a cellular radio-telephone system for Central London. The show is now running at the right length; all that remains is for the editor and the producer to make minor adjustments.

Peter McCann and the radio-telephone system

Looking down on Maggie Philbin weight-lifting

Live programmes, like *Tomorrow's World*, are much more exciting to make than those which are recorded. They are the television equivalent of working without a safety net. Since they rule out any second chances, they call for an alert, clear-headed, decisive approach.

'The British people consume 16000 of these aspirin type pills every minute of every day'

7.30 pm
On the air

The red light is on over the studio door. The director gives instructions to roll the opening film. *Tomorrow's World* is on the air, watched by an audience of up to ten million people.

The edition is a typical mix of items treated briefly but imaginatively; a format devised over many years of experience. Audience research has shown, for example, that medicine is the most popular subject, and this is usually reflected in the running-order. Viewers like gadgets too, and that suits the purpose of the programme: to demonstrate that science and technology not only affect our everyday lives but can also be entertaining. At the same time, *Tomorrow's World* has not been afraid to debunk products making bogus claims.

In the control room. 'We're on the air.'

The SCANNER

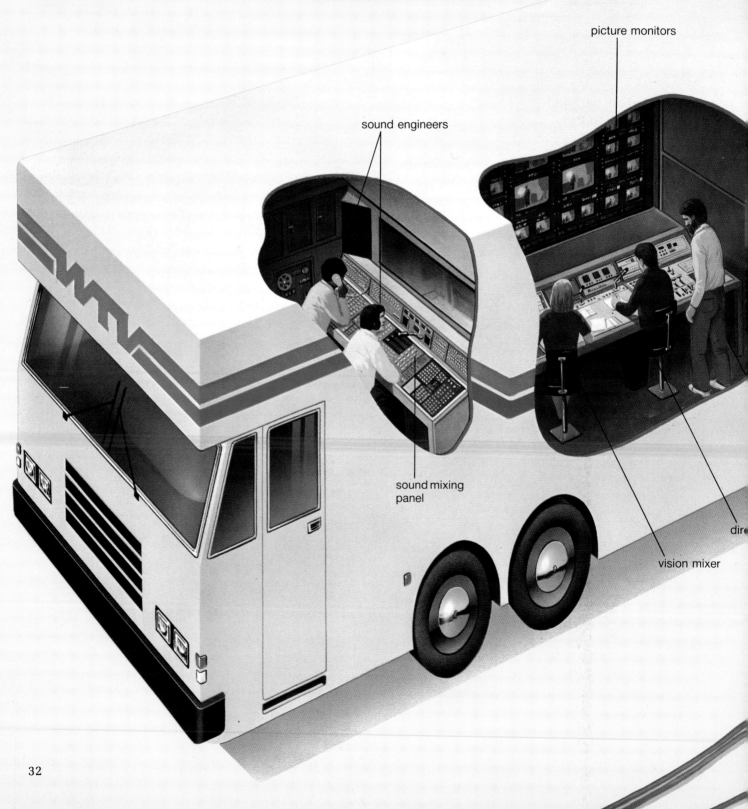

picture monitors

sound engineers

sound mixing panel

vision mixer

dir

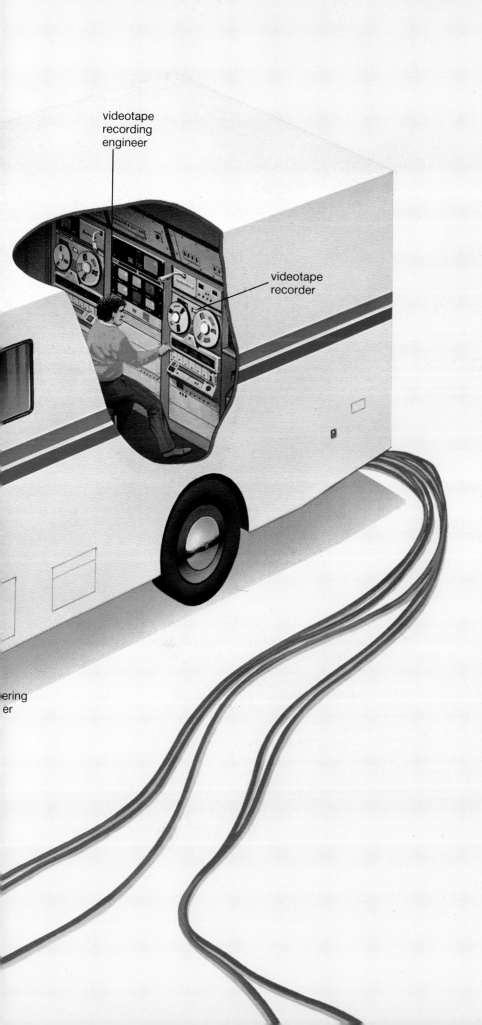

videotape
recording
engineer

videotape
recorder

...ering
...er

An Outside Broadcast is exactly what it sounds like. It is a broadcast from somewhere outside the studio base, using television cameras. Sometimes it is called an 'OB' for short.

The event being televised can be literally anything, from a gardener showing us how to plant a lettuce, to a great royal occasion, involving thousands of people and watched the world over. In fact on page 36 you will see how coverage of the royal wedding was organized.

If you can imagine all the hardware which makes up a single Outside Broadcast unit as a space-fleet, the scanner is the mother-ship. From it, the commander of the fleet, the director, conducts the operation. When there is more than one scanner on site, a producer may be in overall charge.

The main scanner is a large, extremely costly vehicle. The biggest of the breed would not leave you with much change out of £1,500,000.

Inside, in miniature, are all the facilities you would expect to find in a studio gallery. The director sits in a control room, faced by the familiar bank of monitors. Sharing the small space are a production assistant, a vision mixer, and a technical supervisor (engineering manager). A second compartment houses the sound engineer with an assistant. In a third section are the engineers responsible for the technical quality of the pictures, and the VTR operators, who can record the action and play it back.

Without the mother-ship, cameras are blind and microphones are mute. They can only begin to work when they are cabled up to the scanner by a crew of riggers.

Outside Broadcasts 2

SPORT

Outside Broadcast units spend much of their time covering sport. Some events are easier to televise than others. Horse-racing, for instance, makes fewer demands on a director than football because it is more predictable. Horses run in one direction and often on a straight course. It is simply a matter of following their progress. But a footballer who only ran in one direction would soon find himself on the transfer list. During a game, players make intricate patterns and are involved in dramatic incidents, all of which should be captured by the cameras.

The Cup Final

The bigger the match, the more a director has to think about. We will take as an example the Cup Final at Wembley.

Some days before the game, the director goes to the stadium for a survey with an engineering manager. Together they decide how many cameras will be needed and what facilities should be provided for the commentators in their boxes overlooking the terraces. For a European Cup Final there could be as many as forty foreign commentators, each with a microphone and a monitor (a television set showing, in this case, the same pictures as we see at home).

After the survey, all the necessary equipment is driven to Wembley. As we have seen, the flagship is the main scanner. Also in the fleet there may be two smaller scanners and a links vehicle, which passes on the pictures, in the form of micro-waves, from the main scanner to a metal dish mounted on a tower. Their lightning journey then takes them to the headquarters of the television company concerned, before they are relayed to us via our local transmitter.

At Wembley, power is provided by the stadium. If it were not, mobile generators ('gennies') would be used.

The agony and the ecstasy

For a great sporting occasion like the Cup Final, ITV and the BBC between them deploy twenty or more cameras. There is no jockeying for position because the placings have been agreed beforehand. To avoid arguments after the match, the business of who should interview which players or managers has also been worked out in advance – or that is the theory. There have been times when, in the heat of the moment, treaties have been ignored.

If a director has opted for ten cameras, two will be at a fairly high level – 'the best spectator vantage point'. One has a wide-angle lens, taking in all the action, and the other offers a closer version. At pitch-level, a third camera concentrates purely on close-ups, possibly when a goal has been scored or a man fouled. Midway between the high and low positions is a fourth camera which can double for the shots above and below. In addition, there is a camera behind each goal, to catch the agony and the ecstasy in the penalty area, and two more are placed high up, simply for the luxury of slow-motion replays from different angles. The remaining two cameras are in the interview room, where the presenter and the pundits comment on the play.

There is obviously little the director can do by way of rehearsal. On the day of the match there is a technical run-through to see that all the millions of pounds worth of machinery is in working order. After that, the entire production team must be at peak alert to see that no highlight or interesting reaction is missed. Cameramen working in tune with a skilful director can make a good game look even better.

Outside Broadcasts 3

The Royal Wedding

The wedding of the Prince and Princess of Wales called for Independent Television's biggest-ever Outside Broadcast. Five months of planning went into its production. Since the London ITV companies did not have enough facilities to tackle the job on their own, OB units were brought in to help from as far afield as Tyne Tees in Newcastle and HTV in Bristol. The BBC mounted an equally large operation, and cameras from almost every other television-

watching country in the world were also focused on the royal couple.

Within hours of the engagement being announced at the end of February 1981, ITV's co-ordinating producer, Jim Pople, booked a prime site overlooking Westminster Abbey. Two days later it was announced that the wedding would take place at St. Paul's. The guess had not paid off but the news was good. St. Paul's is much more open than the Abbey, giving uninterrupted views.

As soon as the date was confirmed, two researchers were booked to provide a mass of background information for the commentators. Meanwhile the engineering manager made sure that all Thames Television OB units would be available for the occasion, and regional companies were asked to co-operate.

To get to know every detail of the route, the producer walked many times from Buckingham Palace to the Cathedral, working out where the cameras should be placed. Some positions had been used before, including a key vantage point over a chimney-pot on a nine-storey building in Trafalgar Square. In one direction it looks the statue of Lord Nelson in the eye, and in the other it faces straight down the Mall.

The producer finally decided that to cover the processions to and from St. Paul's, the service itself, and the journey in the afternoon from the Palace to Waterloo Station at the start of the royal honeymoon, he would need cameras in sixty positions. Agreement then had to be reached with a number of people, among them the Department of the Environment, officials at the Palace and St. Paul's, owners of private property, the BBC, the American networks, and the police.

Security was obviously of the greatest importance. The names of all those working on the production were sent in for vetting and a system of passes was devised, allowing the bearers into certain areas at certain times.

Twelve ITV scanners would be stationed along the way and the comfort of everyone working in and around them had to be considered. In the vicinity of the Palace alone there would be between two and three hundred technicians. Food tents and field lavatories were set up.

As the months passed, precise timings became vital. In effect the spectacle would consist not just of one procession but of three: first the Queen, Prince Philip, and the Queen

Mother; next Prince Charles with his best man Prince Andrew; and finally the bride. The expected progress of all three had to be finely calculated so that no great moments would be missed.

Each scanner, with anything from two to nine cameras attached, was responsible, under its director, for covering part of the route. The pictures were relayed back to Studio 7 at Thames' Euston headquarters and, from there, beamed to their vast audience.

Even the most thorough planning cannot eliminate bad luck. At a crucial moment during the service in St. Paul's there was a links failure; suddenly screens were blank. 'I aged ten years when the pictures disappeared,' says the producer. Fortunately a deal had been done with the BBC and their shots filled the two minute gap. ITV had agreed to do the same for them.

There was good luck too – for everyone taking part, working or watching. The ITV producer remembers waking up to his alarm call at 5.15 on the morning of the wedding. Dreading rain, he opened the curtains a quarter of an inch and 'Glory be, there wasn't a cloud in the sky. It was the most beautiful day.'

Bird's eye view of camera positions along the Royal Wedding route

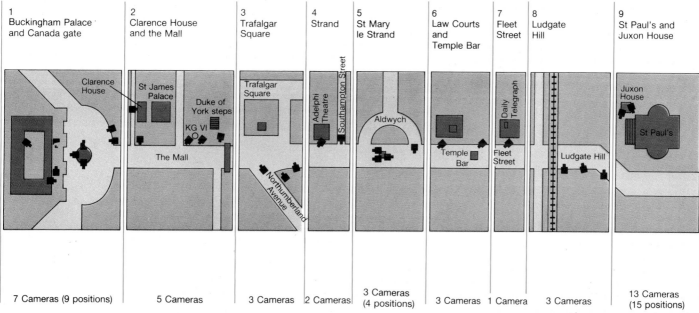

1 Buckingham Palace and Canada gate
Clarence House
7 Cameras (9 positions)

2 Clarence House and the Mall
St James Palace
Duke of York steps
KG VI
The Mall
5 Cameras

3 Trafalgar Square
Trafalgar Square
Northumberland Avenue
3 Cameras

4 Strand
Adelphi Theatre
Southampton Street
2 Cameras

5 St Mary le Strand
Aldwych
3 Cameras (4 positions)

6 Law Courts and Temple Bar
Temple Bar
3 Cameras

7 Fleet Street
Daily Telegraph
Fleet Street
1 Camera

8 Ludgate Hill
Ludgate Hill
3 Cameras

9 St Paul's and Juxon House
Juxon House
St Paul's
13 Cameras (15 positions)

Do-it-yourself television

Television for the people, by the people

We hear quotes from John Lennon, The Who, and George Orwell. We see a middle-class boy playing tennis. Next we are in a factory where a working-class teenager is cutting lengths of timber with a mechanical saw: 'I'm in a dream world when I'm working,' he says. 'One of these days I'll probably cut my hand off.' At a leading public school, Charterhouse, a quiet voice tells us: 'My parents want me to do well and get to a good university.' Again to the teenager slicing timber: 'They've got the pole position up the front and we're left at the back.' These are all thoughts on ambition and the British class system from youngsters taking part in a BBC programme.

Something else

The programme was called *Something Else*. Later, when the kids from different backgrounds are brought together, they have little to say to each other; not because they speak different languages but because they do not have interests in common. The views expressed are thoughtful and honest.

Intimate confessions

Another programme in the same series, *Intimate Confessions*, caused an uproar for taking an equally candid approach to teenage sex. It was a thorough, unashamed examination of the subject, made simply and sensitively. A girl of perhaps seventeen gets home late. From the top of the stairs, her father gives her a telling off, saying how selfish she is and how people will think her 'cheap'. Minutes later, her brother creeps in sheepishly. The tune has changed. His father treats him like a crony from the golf club, calling him a 'lucky devil'. The point is neatly made. Using frank language, both heterosexuals and gays discuss their sexual experiences. There is a joyless poem about masturbation and a lighthearted look at romantic love. Issues which are sometimes sniggered over are brought out into the open.

Street style

Something Else was not just made *for* young people; it was also made *by* young people. That is what access television means. Its aim is to make programmes by, with, and behalf of those about whom decisions are made, rather than with the decision-makers themselves. It belongs to those who are unrepresented, underrepresented, or misrepresented. The words are those of Mike Fentiman who, as head of the BBC Community Programme Unit, has played a big part in the development of do-it-yourself broadcasting.

Something Else was typical of the work of the Unit in that it was compiled by a democratic process. A production panel of a dozen teenagers was recruited from 3,000 applicants. In 1977 a pilot programme was produced entirely under their editorial control. Many months later the experiment bore fruit and the BBC

The Video Box, provided by Channel 4, is the last word in D.I.Y. television. Members of the public are invited to step into a booth and air their views in front of a camera.

JILL WOODS

created room in the schedules for it to expand. The show had what Fentiman calls 'street style', featuring a class of teenager rarely given the chance to have a say on the screen.

The influence of the Unit can be seen in a much greater awareness of the teenage voice across the networks. ITV companies, such as Tyne Tees Television and London Weekend and, to its great credit, Channel Four, have accepted the challenge.

Open Space

Meanwhile, at the BBC, the tradition lives on. A recent run called *Open Space*, chiefly based on ideas sent in by viewers, carried items as diverse as a young Asian actress from Birmingham with a one-woman show about growing up in multi-cultural Britain; a choir of miners from Kent; and a rock band formed by a group of young people suffering from muscular dystrophy.

We are often told that we have the best television service in the world. Certainly in very few countries would a broadcasting channel carry criticism of itself from members of the public. The BBC in its community programmes has often done so, giving air-time to accusations that it has, among other things, shown racist tendencies and that it has been biased towards the right wing when reporting on union affairs.

What do *you* want to see on television?

Cable television can bring more access programming but the omens are not necessarily good. The need to make quick and large profits is likely to squeeze what is called public utility broadcasting out of the reckoning.

If you think it is important that you should be allowed to say exactly what you think on at least some programmes, then it is up to you to act. Write to the companies and tell them what you want to see on the screen. If you are happy to be told what to watch, you have no real grounds for complaint. But if you feel that you have as much right as the professionals to speak your mind on television, you can and must say so.

The Women of Durham Jail

Durham Jail contains about 1,000 male prisoners – and 35 women prisoners. The women are locked up in H Wing. This used to be a maximum security unit for men, but it was closed on the grounds that it was inhumane and unsuitable for long-term imprisonment.

So why is it suitable for women, then? And what kind of women need to be imprisoned behind three sets of bars under 24-hour electronic surveillance? In this programme the women spoke for themselves through their writings and their letters. The women were identified only by their first names and were played by actresses. The picture shows Paola Dionisotti as Jane.

Children Out of Mind

One child in every thousand in Britain today is severely mentally disabled. Because the law requires it, there are special state schools which provide them with the opportunity for development.

Jean Watts is the headteacher of one such school. She made *Children Out of Mind* as 'a personal record of what was a very happy school' – before the local health authority repossessed the building and most of the children were sent away.

One of us

One of us takes a fresh look at the British Raj. How does the former British occupation of India affect today's generation of British-born Asians?

The programme took the form of a funny, one-woman play. It told the story of a star-struck Indian girl from Birmingham who was determined at all costs to become an actress. She and the other characters in her world were all played by Feroza Syal.

Everyone loves a surprise party

THIS IS YOUR LIFE

A helicopter hovers over the River Thames in central London. Among those on board is John Spencer, whose courage in previous operations has earned him the Queen's Award for gallantry. He and the rest of the crew believe that they are taking part in a film promoting the work of the naval rescue service. Below, in a small boat, is a supposed volunteer pretending to be injured and urgently in need of help.

At a signal, Spencer is winched down. To his astonishment, he discovers that the victim is none other than Eamonn Andrews, who announces that 'This is your life, John Spencer.' Accompanied by a police launch, the two of them are taken to the nearest pier and whisked from there by fast car to the studio.

For that dramatic opening, the producer succeeded in getting a section of the Thames closed to traffic from either direction for nearly an hour.

Cut to Rome. Katie Boyle, the well known broadcaster, is in the city to write a fashion piece for a magazine. She has been persuaded to ride in a horse-drawn carriage. Suddenly a policeman orders her driver to halt. Irritated, Ms Boyle protests in fluent Italian, only tailing off when she recognizes, beneath the disguise, the Irish face that launched a thousand intimate tributes.

The scene shifts to Kenya. In a dusty village, not far from Nairobi, the flying doctor is expected for evening surgery. With an assistant at his side, he lands his light aircraft in a clearing. As he steps from the plane, he is greeted by a familiar figure with a red book in his hand. (The red book used on the show itself simply contains the script. Afterwards the subject is presented with a special copy, complete with photographs, and a videotape of the programme.) While the assistant takes over his medical duties, the flying doctor is driven to the airport where he is escorted on to a flight for London. When he has had a few hours sleep at a hotel, his story is told for British viewers and he hurries back home to look after his patients.

The pick-up
Those are all actual examples of what the *This is Your Life* team call 'the pick-up' – the often emotional moment when the famous and the unknown alike learn, to their amazement and sometimes genuine shock, that they are to be the subject of the programme. Only one nominee, Danny Blanchflower, has so far absolutely refused to co-operate. Confronted by the host, he made it plain that he preferred to keep his life to himself.

The enduring format was devised by Ralph Edwards. It was a big hit in

The research

The next step is to enlist the support of partners, relatives, and friends. It is obviously essential to make sure that the subjects will be in the country and available on the projected dates. Once their presence is guaranteed, barring last minute crises, the pick-up can be planned, while researchers discreetly probe the life in question. From the mass of material which they compile, the producer and the writers will later decide what to include in the show.

Gathering information may take several months, although there are times when subjects hit the headlines overnight and have to be investigated in a matter of days. On occasion the entire effort is wasted. One celebrity was denied his chance to appear by his six-year old grandson. Hearing his grandfather break off from a telephone conversation to call through to the kitchen: 'Barbara, are we free next Wednesday night to go out to supper?', the child unwittingly blurted: 'No, grandad, you're on *This is Your Life!*' Grandad had no option but to ring the producer and admit what had happened. The programme was cancelled.

But usually the system remains watertight. Some people find the results embarrassing. They maintain that it is unfair to reveal in public the private lives of unsuspecting men and women. Nevertheless, most viewers clearly enjoy the 'surprise party'. Which side are you on?

America before being taken up in Britain, first by the BBC and later by Thames Television. For many years it has been one of the most popular programmes on the network. Why? In the view of its highly experienced writers, who also act as consultants, the answer is that 'Everyone loves a surprise party.' Everyone except Danny Blanchflower, that is.

The code-name

Keeping the surprise a secret can be a major headache. Once subjects have been chosen, they are given a code name (Diamond, Air, Water, Pigeon, Diva, and Fox have all been used) by which they will be known in conversations and correspondence.

The production team

The planning meeting

I watch Miami Vice because of the hunky guys and the up-to-date music. Dallas occasionally. It just torments me, Dallas, 'cos it's so ridiculous.

I watch Horizon because it goes into things in depth.

I've always watched Coronation Street and Crossroads. I like Emmerdale Farm – it's natural. And I like Nature programmes.

I watch Dynasty and Dallas, and I don't watch Coronation Street. I like films, any films.

Ratings and critics

Sweating it out

Promote yourself to the rank of television producer. It is 8.58 pm on a Tuesday evening. A programme which you have been working on for many weeks has just been shown to the British public. If you have been brave enough to watch with friends or family, you may ask for their comments. But the most important question still nags you. How big was the national audience and what was its reaction? In a theatre you could put yourself out of your misery at once by listening to the applause and seeing how many tickets were sold. In television you have to sweat it out until the ratings are published.

If the viewing figures are important to the individual producer, they are much more so to the company for which he or she works. In the case of the BBC, a consistently poor showing against the commercial opposition will make the Government very reluctant to increase the licence fee. In ITV, the money comes not from the State (as we have seen elsewhere in the book) but from selling screen time to advertisers. If the ratings reveal that ITV is not attracting enough viewers, those advertisers may not be tempted to buy any time at all – at least not at the asking price.

To begin with, the BBC and ITV each had their own method of measuring the audience. The result was that although they were both doing the same sums, they were tending to arrive at different answers. BBC research would put the BBC in the lead and ITV research would claim victory for ITV. Seeing the confusion, the Annan Committee on broadcasting made a sensible suggestion: Why not get together and produce a single set of figures? It may sound like a perfectly obvious solution to you but in fact the joint operation took years to set up.

BARB

The Broadcasters' Audience Research Board (BARB for short) opened for business in 1981. It is owned equally by the BBC and ITV. The governing board is made up of three members from each organization and an independent chairman. BARB has only four full-time employees; its research is done by another company called Audits of Great Britain (AGB).

It is clearly not possible to be in regular contact with every single viewer; even if it were, the cost would be enormous. Instead a 'panel' of 3,000 homes has been chosen to represent all of us. These homes are picked with great care to represent a perfect cross-section of the population and the various regions of Britain. Among the factors taken into account are the number of people in the home, social class, the age and job of the head of the household, whether there is more than one television set, whether the second set is a portable, and whether there is a video cassette recorder.

Each home on the panel is fitted with a meter, connected to all the television sets in the house. The meter records when each set is in use, which channel has been selected, and the times of switching on and off. It can also tell when something other than a broadcast programme is on the screen, for example, a video game or a computer read-out.

To help the meter count how many members of the household are actually watching, the panel-homes are all issued with an electronic 'pad' on which there are eight numbered buttons. Everyone living in the house is given a number, so that it might go like this: mother = one, father = two, eldest son = three, and so on. And if grandma comes for the weekend, she will share in the allocation as well. The family and visitors simply press their buttons every time they start and stop viewing.

The information from the push-button pads goes into the meters which are 'interrogated' each night by the AGB computer.

Pooling this mass of detail and scaling it up gives BARB a minute-by-minute indication of what we watch.

League tables

When all the elements have been fed into the AGB computer and processed, the patterns of our viewing habits emerge. At the simplest level, we know which have been the most popular programmes of the week, channel by channel, and these eagerly awaited league tables are provided free of charge to the newspapers. Those who, like advertisers, want a much more detailed breakdown, pay for the service. In return for their subscription they get a weekly report about an inch thick which gives analyses of audiences in every area, for every programme.

Those who fill and sell space on television can learn a little from two more sources. The first is a BBC system whereby, on behalf of BARB, viewers are asked to enter their opinions of what they watch in a daily diary. The second response is from the professional critics. Some use their columns to tell their readers more about themselves than about the shows they have seen. Others are sometimes able to pinpoint strengths and weaknesses.

I watch Miami Vice and the News and that's about it. And the weather in the summer.

So you want to be a TV critic?

If you are a film or theatre critic, you are writing about something that only a limited number of people besides you will have seen. When you are a television critic, you write about something that millions of people besides you will have seen, and they all have views, they are all armchair critics. And your review will be published *after*, not before they have seen the programme, so you do not influence them. All this makes life difficult for a TV critic.

What makes a good critic? For a start you have to enjoy television. Above all, you have to communicate your own enthusiasm for a programme to other people. Most critics have firm opinions, and whether they like or dislike a programme they can always say why, and pick on the details. You must also be informative, describing clearly what programmes are about, and you have to be entertaining; if you are not, your column will fail to attract readers. A good critic will communicate in the same way that you would talk to someone who is sitting right next to you – there is no need for jargon or high-flown English.

Do you have to stay in every night watching television? Before the arrival of video, TV critics did have a problem if there was a clash between going out and watching a programme. But now video has changed their lives. They can switch on their recorder, set it to a fixed time, and go out.

Critics on provincial newspapers usually watch on their own set. London critics are regularly invited to previews. These may be on a big screen in a preview theatre, or sometimes the TV company will show them on an ordinary television set in a studio. The problem with watching just previews is that very often the big television companies will only show the programmes they particularly want you to see. If you view on your own set, then you can write about the run-of-the-mill programmes that the public watches. And you can even review the weather forecasts or the ads.

On the whole if you are a critic you can choose what you cover. Different critics have different interests and enthusiasms, though they have to be careful not to inflict what could be their own specialized fancies on the general public. Critics writing a weekly column, dealing with a variety of programmes, will try to give a personal impression of what they watch in the hope that it will mirror what the general public has seen. Critics write to a deadline and to a fixed number of words. They do not necessarily come in to the office very often, but their copy does. They can send it by post, leave it at the reception desk, or phone it in, when it will be taken down by a copy-taker.

If it's too political, I'm not interested at all. I watch Dallas and Dynasty, but not every week because I don't need to.

I watch opera because it lends itself to TV. And Criterium cycle racing – that's *very* good on TV.

Try it yourself

Suggest to a couple of friends that you all watch the same programme and write, say, 100 words (about 10 lines) about it. See how your opinions differ. And remember, be readable and entertaining. If you like or dislike something, be prepared to say why. And above all communicate your enthusiasm.

Commercial Break 2

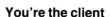

Getting the message across

You're the client

Imagine for a moment that you are the boss of a big company which has just produced a new kind of cassette player, smaller and cheaper than the others on the market. Naturally you want to tell the world about it and to sell as many as you possibly can.

First you have to decide how much you can afford to spend on launching the product. Next, you instruct your executives to pick the best advertising agency for the job. From now on you will be known as 'the client'.

After talking and testing and racking their brains, the agency will tell you how and where they think the advertising should be presented. They might suggest posters, displays in shops, give-away offers, competitions, big spreads in the press, and so on. But almost certainly the spearhead of the attack will be one or more television commercials, for reasons we saw earlier in the book. Your brand manager will examine the proposals and call for changes wherever necessary.

The look

The agency will now hand the project over to their creative department, who may say that it has all been done before, or that it cannot be done for the money, or how about doing it this way? Finally an idea for a commercial

will be agreed, with a writer and producer in charge of shaping and shooting. They in turn will hire a production company and a good director to give them the 'look' they want. Some of the best British directors of commercials, Alan Parker and Ridley Scott, for example, have gone on to great success in the film industry.

At this stage you, the client, will be given an estimated bill – a budget telling you how much the whole exercise will cost you. A careful agency will also make absolutely sure that you know where the commercial will be shot, who is in it, what they will say, what clothes they will wear, and how the cassette player will appear. The more you know from the start, the less you will be justified in complaining later. You, or your team, will be consulted on the object of each brief scene. Does it get the message across? Is it confusing? Can it be improved?

The action

There comes a point when the talking has to make way for action. Viewers often wonder why a film unit has to go all the way to Nassau simply to take pictures of, say, a model holding a bottle of shampoo. The answer is probably that there is no cheaper way of getting a different-looking, exotic

background with guaranteed sun. Southport has its charms but agencies might argue that it would not set off a particular product to advantage. All the same, even in the Bahamas, it is possible to spot a commercial film crew waiting days or even weeks for a clear blue sky.

When commentary and music have been added to the edited film, or videotape, the agency will be anxious to see your reaction to their work. If, together, you have got it right, you should be able to sit back and watch the sales graph of your new cassette player climb steeply.

What do *you* think?

For all its effectiveness – or rather because of its effectiveness – some people believe that television advertising is a bad thing. They say that it persuades viewers to buy items which they do not need or cannot afford. Notably at Christmas time, commercials featuring games and toys come thick and fast during afternoon programming. Manufacturers and agencies are obviously counting on children to put pressure on their parents. For their part the advertisers would reply that viewers have free will and that no one is forcing them to buy anything. What do *you* think?

HOW THEY ADVERTISED THE POWER PACKET

THE PRODUCT~ THE 'POWER PACKET'. IT'S THE SMALLEST AND CHEAPEST PERSONAL STEREO EVER.

THE MANUFACTURER~ E.M.C. ELECTRONICS. THEY'RE THE TALLEST AND SLEEKEST STEREO MAKERS EVER.

HI!

HI! ER...

HIGHEST!

THE MANUFACTURER WANTS TO ADVERTISE HIS NEW PRODUCT, SO FROM A NUMBER OF ADVERTISING AGENCIES HE SELECTS ONE.

THIS ONE.

APRIL

DOLITTLE GRABBIT & RUNN ADVERTISING AGENTS

THE AGENCY CALLS THE MANUFACTURER ITS 'CLIENT'. IT TAKES HIS PRODUCT AND RESEARCHES IT BY QUESTIONING THE 'TARGET CONSUMERS'.

? ?

WITH THIS INFORMATION THE AGENCY PLANS A CAMPAIGN. IT DECIDES WHAT 'MEDIA' IT WILL USE, IE. POSTERS, PRESS, SHOP DISPLAYS OR TV.

Power Pa... I'M NOT AT ALL SURE ABOUT TV ON THIS ONE...

THE AGENCY THEN OUTLINES ITS PLANS TO THE CLIENT.

...AND, OF COURSE, TV.

PROPOSALS FOR POWER PACKET ADS

THE CLIENT MIGHT MAKE SUGGESTIONS OR CHANGES. ALL THIS INFORMATION IS THEN GIVEN TO THE AGENCY'S CREATIVE DEPARTMENT. THEY WILL CREATE THE IDEAS THAT WILL SELL THE POWER PACKET.

HOWBOUT...

UH HUH, WELL LET ME JUST RUN THIS ONE UP A FLAGPOLE....

I'VE GOT IT!!

I'VE HAD IT.

THE AGENCY PRESENTS ITS IDEAS TO THE CLIENT.

IN THE TV AD WE'LL HAVE CLINT EASTWOOD DO THIS BIT....

WOW.

HE APPROVES THEM.

I APPROVE THEM.

AT THIS STAGE THE AGENCY IS READY TO FILM THE AD AND 'PRE-PRODUCTION' STARTS. THAT MEANS IT CHOOSES A FILM COMPANY, A DIRECTOR, A CAST AND A LOCATION.

BAHAMAS HOTELS BARS BEACHES BARS MORE BARS

NOT AGAIN.

THE FILM IS SHOT.

I CAN'T FIND THE POXY POWER PACKET ANYWHERE...

PITY CLINT WAS TOO BUSY.

THE RESULTING FILM GOES FOR 'POST-PRODUCTION', IE. EDITING, VOICE AND MUSIC DUBBING, AND COLOUR GRADING.

NICE TAN!

THE FINAL FILM IS PRESENTED TO THE CLIENT..... HE LIKES IT.

I LIKE IT.

FILLS YOUR EARS WITHOUT EMPTYING YOUR POCKETS

THE AGENCY 'BUYS TIME' ON SEVERAL COMMERCIAL BREAKS AND SENDS VIDEO COPIES OF THE FILM TO THE TV STATIONS.

COMMERCIAL: POWER PACKET

THE PUBLIC SEES THE AD. THEY LIKE IT.

LIKE IT.

FILLS YOUR EA...

THE CLIENT GETS HIS FIRST SALES FIGURES. HE LIKES THEM.

POWER PACKET   SALES

LOVE IT!!

ED CARR

TOP OF THE POPS ▶

The beat goes on

Swinging London

Few shows have a history as long as that of *Top of the Pops*. It started in black and white in 1964. The first compere was Jimmy Savile. Among the stars he introduced on the opening night were The Beatles, The Rolling Stones, and Cliff Richard.

That was the decade when the capital was called 'swinging London'. A short, ordinary alley – Carnaby Street – became world famous; a sort of symbol of a new freedom that seemed to be in the air. The contraceptive pill became freely available, fashion was fun, working-class youngsters with talent found that they could be successful, and England won the World Cup. It was like spring after a long winter. And pop music echoed what was happening.

You provide the chocolates

In May 1983, more than nineteen years after its birth, Top of the Pops celebrated one thousand performances. It has lasted because the contents are, in effect, chosen by the viewers themselves. 'They provide the chocolates', says a producer, 'and we do the packaging.' He means that the programme simply reflects the ups and downs of the

Jimmy Savile introducing the first-ever *Top of the Pops* on 1 January 1964

The dancers rehearsing

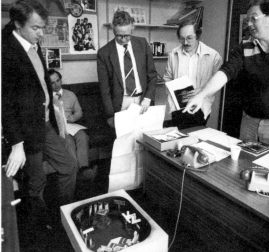

'How are we going to fit everyone into this small set?'

record charts and they in turn show which numbers the public likes best in any given week.

Nowadays the charts are compiled by computer, showing sales figures from selected record shops throughout the country. The results are published on Tuesday morning, when the *Top of the Pops* producer must decide which bands or solo artistes to include in the line-up. There is no secret about the rules of selection. They are printed for anyone to see. Here are some of them as they appear in a BBC handout:

Titles only played when in 75 and going up the charts.

Yo-yo titles only included when higher than previous chart placings.

No title (other than the Number 1 placing) ever included on consecutive weeks.

Second play preference now given to self-contained groups (i.e. those not containing session musicians).

There is never a guarantee of a second play unless in Top 10.

If a title has first been played outside the Top 30, it will never be included again until in the Top 30.

In case you were puzzled by the mention of session musicians, they are freelance professional musicians often hired by bands to make them sound bigger or better.

Precise guidelines are also laid down about the use of backing tracks – music recorded elsewhere to which performers will mime.

Wherever possible, singers and musicians are encouraged to come in person to the Television Centre, but videos have become too ingenious and tempting to resist. The best of them represent some of the most imaginative work television has to offer.

A carnival atmosphere

On programme day, a *Top of the Pops* director is lucky if the schedule allows half an hour in which to rehearse a band. The same group might have just returned from Sri Lanka with an expensive and exciting video. Which would you prefer to include in the show – a straightforward performance shot within the tight limitations of the studio? or a series of colourful, exotic

'This costume doesn't fit.'

images illustrating the music? Nevertheless, especially when the programme is transmitted live, the studio has a carnival atmosphere. Look at the photos and judge for yourself.

A successful appearance on *Top of the Pops* can mean instant stardom. Research has shown that as well as attracting a large audience at the time of broadcasting, it is also the programme that families most like to record at home. So, thanks to the video revolution, the beat goes on, and on, and on. . . .

Applause, applause

Walking into the *Top of the Pops* studio, you would never think that the show had been carefully rehearsed all day. It obviously has to be, otherwise the six cameras would be colliding like bumper cars, not knowing where to go next. But forgetting the television hardware for a moment, you could easily imagine that you had just joined a lively party in a big discotheque.

Everywhere there are coloured lights, revolving and swivelling overhead, framing the side panels, and glowing up through the stages where the bands will perform.

On the stairways and catwalks, on the floor itself, the invited guests dance to the rhythm relayed over loudspeakers. Wearing a liberty of styles, from gypsy to jungle chic, ribbons to Rasta, and crowned with paper hats, they hurl streamers across the crowd.

The Rolling Stones
in the first *Top of the Pops*

Singers get a brief introduction from a disc jockey. Dancers who double as cheerleaders mingle with the fancy dressers, urging them to clap. Applause, applause. Familiar voices to a familiar beat. Applause, applause. Parting the knots of onlookers, the cameras swoop and glide, homing in on the shots called for by the director. Applause, applause.

Into the chart sequence, recorded in the afternoon. The studio presenters rattle through the British top forty, seemingly all in one breath. Two or three pauses for songs, one of them a video on a huge screen. A girl with cropped, copper hair is sitting at a keyboard in a field. The grass turns to waves of barley, then the sea. By the time it ends, the dancers are high on a rostrum, tightly linked in steps and patterns. Finally 'it's number one; it's top of the pops'. A show where the first shall be last. Another band; another glint in the glass eye of the music industry. And time to say goodnight. Applause, applause.

How do you get in?
The chosen few who get in to see the show, 106 of them per week, should be between 16 and 24 years old. They must also be very patient. It is simply a matter of writing to the BBC Ticket Unit, waiting and hoping. The address is at the end of the book.

Teletext

Reading your television set

In the ancient world, the famous oracle at Delphi was a priestess who was believed to be a mouthpiece of the gods. After three days of fasting, followed by a light snack of laurel leaves, she would go into a trance and answer questions put to her by perplexed pilgrims.

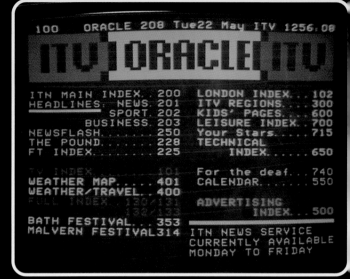

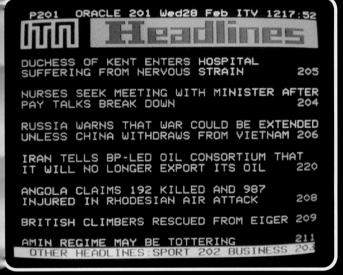

Tapping the election results into Ceefax

Oracle and Ceefax

The modern Oracle has several advantages over its classical counterpart. To begin with, you do not have to travel anywhere for consultations. It simply sits in the corner of the room, disguised as a television set. It can deal with dozens of queries in a matter of seconds and survives on a diet of electricity.

Oracle, which stands for Optional Reception of Announcements by Coded Line Electronics, is the ITV teletext service. Like the TV Times it is owned jointly by the ITV companies. Its development (and that of its BBC equivalent, Ceefax) can be traced to the nineteen sixties. In that decade, engineers on both channels started to look into the possibilities of subtitling programmes for the deaf and, much more ambitiously, of printing newspapers in the homes of viewers.

Permission was given by the Home Office for a trial period in 1974, and the next year a very few, very expensive sets were able to receive experimental teletext broadcasts. Finally, in 1977, Oracle became generally available to those prepared to pay for it. Soon, all new sets will be equipped to display teletext.

The system, which is a British invention, takes advantage of the fact that of the 625 horizontal lines which make up a television picture, twenty-five or so are not used. Initially, Oracle had to be content with two of the redundant lines. Gradually the allocation grew, and the logical outcome is a channel (or channels) devoted entirely to teletext. With a full 625 lines to play with, tens of thousands of pages of information can be offered for instant viewing.

The material seen on Oracle comes from two sources. A special unit at the London headquarters of ITN is responsible for the news, sport, and business news. The rest of the output (which includes subtitles, programme schedules, weather, features, theatre and events details, travel news, consumer items, gossip, pop charts, film reviews, sections for children, and so on) is compiled at the heart of the Oracle operation in the West End.

The Oracle newsroom

Transmission equipment

At lightning speed

The text, which is typed on keyboards, is revealed on visual display units as it passes into the vast memory bank of the computer. A lightning journey then takes it via the Post Office Tower to a rendezvous with transmitting television signals and into our homes.

The speed with which Oracle and Ceefax can receive and dispatch any item is one of their chief strengths. Let us suppose that news comes in of the assassination of a Head of State. In a radio or television newsroom, decisions would have to be made about treatment and timing before a script could be typed, agreed, and read by a presenter, who would probably interrupt a programme. On Oracle or Ceefax, a researcher could assess the story, type it directly on to the screen, and have it on the air literally within seconds.

Teletext is popular with advertisers. Reaching an audience of millions, who are reading their television sets rather than merely watching them, it offers an attentive market place. Graphics, which began by being relatively crude, are rapidly becoming slicker and more animated.

Of those two targets of the nineteen sixties which we touched on earlier – subtitling for the deaf and printing home newspapers – the first, at least, has been partially reached. Many hours a week of television broadcasting now offer subtitles and more will follow. Cost is an important factor. It takes one person roughly one week to subtitle one hour of programming.

Do you want it?

The second target is still some way off. The technology exists; the question is: does anyone want it? By pressing a remote control button, we can get a television set to print out a copy of the text shown on the screen. It is therefore perfectly possible to produce an entire newspaper by the same method. For the Fleet Street barons, the prospect is not a happy one. The verdict will rest with the viewer – and the trade unions.

More immediately, as costs tumble, sets are being fitted with larger 'brains' which will allow us to choose from a huge variety of electronic games and puzzles, as well as greatly expanded teletext services. Sets which respond to our voices will also be able to consult Oracle, Ceefax, or a rival system, decide which programmes are to our liking and automatically record them.

Who knows, perhaps, like the oracle at Delphi, the set will one day answer back.

Job spot

Oracle prefers those who have done a National Council for the Training of Journalists course and who have newspaper experience.

One of the last photographs ever taken by Lee Lyon

Filming in the Wild

SURVIVAL

The teams who film *Wildlife* are probably the toughest breed in television. They often have to live in harsh conditions for weeks on end and sometimes take necessary risks. But courage is not enough. The team must also be patient, skilful and able to improvise. How would you get close to a flock of shy pelicans, for instance? Dieter Plage solved the problem by borrowing a stuffed pelican from a department of zoology and hiding a camera in it. He then mounted the strange creature on a plump inner tube and by pushing it in front of him, got within yards of the cruising birds.

Cameramen like Dieter Plage and Alan Root have become legends on *Survival*. According to Colin Willock, who helped to create the programme, in other times they might have been adventurers or fighter pilots. 'In Alan', he wrote, 'exists a compulsion to put one foot over the rim of every available precipice.' Root has had many lucky escapes, among them an underwater brush with an enraged hippo. The animal bit him on the backside and then sank its teeth into his calf, leaving him with a wound big enough to push a Coca-Cola bottle through.

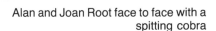
Alan and Joan Root face to face with a spitting cobra

The women in the *Survival* family have been just as brave as the men. Refusing to be put off by a scorpion bite on her wedding night, Joan Root has shared danger with her husband, notably in the first hot-air balloon flight over the twenty thousand foot summit of Mount Kilimanjaro.

In 1975 the programme suffered a tragic loss. The victim was Lee Lyon, a young Californian. She was making a film about elephant calves being air-lifted from a swamp to Kagera National Park in Rwanda. By hanging head first from the helicopter under which they were slung, she managed to get some marvellous pictures of the elephants. But as she covered their unloading at the other end, one of them charged unexpectedly and crushed her. The edited film became her memorial. It was called, simply, 'Lee's Story'.

Highly experienced cameramen and camerawomen, dotted around the globe, are the spearhead of *Survival*. Colin Willock has called them: 'a specialist fighting force in constant and close contact with the enemy and often operating far behind enemy lines'. But troops are useless without leadership and direction. On *Survival* these are largely provided by the writers, who are also naturalists. They begin the process with a story treatment – a guide which tells the cameraman what the show is about and how it can best be illustrated. As the film arrives back at base in Park Lane, the writer views it and decides what to use and what to reject. The unused material is carefully catalogued and stored in a library which now contains many millions of feet.

Next the writer prepares another treatment, this time for the film editor. It will describe in fine detail how the remaining footage should be assembled. The result, which may take three weeks, is known as a rough-cut. This early version may still be ten minutes too long but it allows the team to make adjustments and to see where they went wrong. From the

Dieter Plage with a baby orang-utang who wants to be in the movies

lessons learned, a fine-cut is produced.

At this stage the show is silent ('mute'). Natural history cameramen have far too much to think about to record sound along with all their pictures. So every single effect, from faint footsteps to roars, has to be found and laid on a separate track to synchronize with the images.

If music is called for, decisions must be made about whether to use existing work or to have a score specially written and recorded. When that has been added, the dubbing

mixer will blend in the commentary spoken by a narrator.

Since its black and white beginning in 1961, *Survival* has been a big hit for Anglia Television. The founder of the programme, Aubrey Buxton, wanted to bring natural history to a wider audience. He could hardly have dreamed that the show would sell in over a hundred countries. On the way, it has won international prizes galore and the Queen's Award to Industry for its foreign earnings. More importantly, with other wildlife programmes, it has helped to open our eyes.

Alan Root feeding Sally the hippo in Naivasha, Kenya

Alan Root filming wildebeeste

The BBC Open University Production Centre on the campus at Walton Hall in Milton Keynes

Graham McGrath as Hansel in *Hansel and Gretel – What does the Tale Tell?* This is part of a series of programmes for the Open University's course on Purpose and Planning in the Curriculum.

The Open University

The university of the second chance

As long ago as 1927, the *Radio Times* was mentioning the idea of a 'University of the Air' but Britain had to wait nearly forty years before anything came of it.

Getting started

The man who is generally given the credit for getting the Open University off the ground is Sir Harold Wilson. He had begun to think about it even before he became leader of the Labour party. In the early nineteen sixties, he told a party conference what he had in mind: 'It's designed to provide an opportunity for those who for one reason or another have not been able to take advantages of higher education, now to do so.'

To us it seems an obviously fair and worthwhile project, but at the time many important people, including officials at the Department of Education, were not enthusiastic. When he became Prime Minister in 1964, Harold Wilson gave one of his

Ministers, Jennie Lee, the job of winning the battle for an Open University. With the help of some powerful allies, she did just that.

Originally Jennie Lee wanted the whole of a fourth television channel to be given to the scheme, but that was rejected. When the matter was raised with ITV, their reaction, according to Lord Goodman who played a leading part in negotiations, '. . . was very simple . . . they hadn't a moment of time for it. Their revenue depended upon advertisements and they didn't see discussions about geometry producing a very large advertising response.' (It should be remembered, though, that ITV had been first with Schools Television.) In the end the BBC, under its Director-General Sir Hugh Greene, agreed to the use of BBC2. A Planning Committee was set up and when its report was accepted by the Government, the ambitious newcomer was ready for take-off.

The second chance

The Open University, which received its Royal Charter in 1969, now has its headquarters at Milton Keynes. Jennie Lee wanted it to be 'a university of the second chance but not of the second best'. Since the first teaching year in 1971, more than 50,000 students have taken advantage of that second chance by earning their degrees. They are ordinary men and women who, through no fault of their own, were not able to graduate earlier in their lives. What makes them different from other students, apart from their average age, is that they do their university work in their own homes and in their own time. They do not go to lessons or lectures; their lessons are brought to them – on television, radio, video and audio cassettes, and in print.

Because most of the students are busy making a living or looking after a family, or both, the programmes specially designed for them are

broadcast in the early morning, at teatime, late in the evening, and at weekends.

In any given year some 90,000 students are enrolled at Milton Keynes. There are 130 undergraduate courses for them to choose from, shared among six faculties: Arts, Educational Studies, Social Sciences, Science, Technology, and Mathematics. Under the heading Continuing Education there are also separate non-degree courses ranging from broad areas, like how to bring up a baby, to more specialized knowledge, such as guidance on drug therapy for doctors.

The first of its kind

This impressive place of learning, the first of its kind in the world, is a partnership between the Open University and the BBC. It has all the modern broadcasting facilities of the most up-to-date radio and television stations. In its self-contained studios, sixty-five BBC producers, chosen chiefly for their academic ability, work with the support of a technical, design and engineering staff numbering over three hundred. They make about 250 television programmes a year, as well as 400 radio programmes. These are watched and heard not only by Open University students but by undergraduates and staff in other universities and in sixth forms throughout the United Kingdom. They may well have helped to raise overall educational standards.

Just because the Open University came on the scene many centuries after Oxford and Cambridge does not mean that the degrees it offers are in any way inferior. You could say that they demand even more discipline; they can call for six years' hard labour – twelve hours a week, thirty-two weeks a year. And that has to be fitted in with other responsibilities both at home and at work. The 'university of the second chance' has proved itself to be first rate.

Film editing

Feature films on television

Twice a year, in spring and winter, the programme buyers for the BBC and ITV set off on a shopping trip to Hollywood. They have millions of pounds to spend.

During a week of intensive viewing they compete for the best series offered by the three American networks. Dashing from one darkened screening room to another, the buyers are ready to act fast. When they see a show which they think will attract a large British audience, they must make a bid without delay. A $3,000,000 deal was once done with a stubby pencil and a scrap of paper on the wall of the Beverly Wilshire Hotel. However, the networks realize that their clients have travelled thousands of miles to do business and they try to make the competition as civilized as possible.

The visiting executives will also be on the lookout for feature films. Usually these can be shown on television three years after their release in the cinema. Hammered out in a spell of hard bargaining, a typical contract might allow the BBC or ITV to screen a film three times in a period of seven years.

The bill can be sizeable. *Gone With the Wind*, for instance, cost the BBC $9,000,000, while ITV had to go to $10,000,000 for a package which included the two *Jaws* pictures.

ITV complain that the prices are too high but they say that while the BBC can afford blockbusters out of its licence money, advertisers will expect the commercial companies to follow suit.

The signs are that in future Hollywood may have to settle for less. There is no longer any guarantee that a film which was popular in the cinema will be equally successful on television. In any case, it can hardly be expected to notch up enormous viewing figures when it is shown for the second and third times. Cable television and video, with a choice of brand new titles, also reduce the demand for older productions.

Once films have been acquired, either outright or just for an agreed period, decisions have to be made. As they stand, are the pictures suitable for showing to a mass television audience? Do they contain scenes which could be disturbing for younger viewers? Depending on the answers, a picture which has already been passed by the British Board of Film Censors may be re-censored for the home.

The system is open to question. There have been rare examples where cuts made for television have seriously interfered with the intentions of the makers. While this must be infuriating for writers and directors, the attitude of the broadcasting companies is understandable. Since they cannot know who is watching, they feel they have a duty to protect viewers who may be upset or offended. On the other side of the coin, some films have been shown in longer versions on television than in the cinema. The

reason is that in the period since their first release, public ideas about what is shocking have become more relaxed.

In recent years, television companies (notably Channel Four) have started to repay their debt to the film industry by investing in features which can be shown both in the cinema and on the small screen. This long overdue move has given young film-makers a chance and has produced some superb work.

STUNTS

A perilous way to make a living

In the days of silent films, action was everything. The more they saw their heroes and heroines leaping off cliffs, rooftops, planes, cars, and horses, the more audiences liked it. They expected something exciting to look at and producers were happy to oblige.

Risking your life

For a while stars often did their own stunts; then it was realized that if they were injured, production would have to be held up – and time was money. Stuntmen and women, doubling for the leading actors, have risked their lives to thrill the paying customers ever since.

Some of the great names in stunting had learned their trade either in other forms of entertainment or in the forces. In the 1920s a number of American pilots, who had survived the dogfights of the First World War, set up as barnstormers – touring the

United States with death-defying displays of daredevil flying. When they were recruited by the cinema, a new form of aerial spectacular was created. Nerveless men and women would transfer from the wing of one aircraft to the wing of another in mid-air, hampered by the wind which struck them at gale force. They would even dangle at the end of rope ladders to sweep distressed damsels from the roofs of moving trains.

Yakima Canutt

The legendary Yakima Canutt came from an equally dangerous background. From 1917–24 he held the title of World Champion All Round Cowboy for his skill with bucking broncos and stubborn steers. The experience stood him in good stead when he was signed up by Hollywood. In *Stagecoach*, for example, he was able to recreate a

stunt he had perfected on the rodeo circuit. We see a coach, pulled by six horses, being driven across a desert. Canutt rides up and jumps from his own mount to the leading pair. He then falls between the galloping hooves, lets the coach pass over him, runs after it, manages to haul himself back aboard, tussles with the driver, leaps on to the horses and Roman-rides his way once again to the first pair. Apart from the fact that the team was not travelling quite as fast as it appears to in the film, the sequence owes nothing to trickery and everything to the agility, timing, and courage of Yakima Canutt.

The coming of television provided more work for stuntmen and women, but the medium has not, on the whole, used them to such good effect. The cinema can afford to lavish more money and time on its action. The chariot race in the 1959 version of *Ben*

Hur, for instance, took Canutt and his assistants five months to prepare. In that period, television would have transmitted forty episodes of *Coronation Street*.

Alf Joint

Even so, the small screen has certainly had its moments of stunting glory, some of them in commercials. Veteran stuntman Alf Joint created one when he was filmed delivering a box of chocolates to a yacht anchored in the Mediterranean. Before you think to yourself 'Some people have all the luck.' wait a moment; just to add spice to the otherwise simple mission, Joint was asked to do it the hard way. Would he please dive from a clifftop and swim to the vessel? Since stuntmen are not paid to say No, he very soon found himself peering down at the target. He estimated the distance to the surface of the sea at about eighty feet. He was only half right. In the event his perfect dive was measured at just under one hundred and sixty feet. And that was not the end of the story. The director asked for a 'Take two'. As a result of the second dive, Joint was taken to hospital for treatment to his injuries. The actor for whom he had been doubling climbed aboard the yacht unscathed at the end of the commercial, his box of chocolates apparently watertight. The beautiful woman with a sweet tooth, languishing on deck, was suitably impressed.

Why do they do it?

The art of stunting is to make the action look dangerous, while taking as few risks as possible. Nevertheless, it remains a perilous way to earn a living. No precaution is fail-safe. Even the cardboard boxes used to break a fall can fracture bones if they are struck at the wrong angle. An American stuntman, A.J. Bakunis, was killed when the airbag he was relying on to cushion his fall split as he landed on it from a height of three hundred and fifteen feet. Chairs made of balsa wood and windows of heavy, brittle plastic improve the odds in fight scenes, as does body-padding, but the chances of a mishap would still not be acceptable to most of us.

Why do stuntmen and women do it? Novelty, glory, artistry – they all give different answers. But now, more than ever, the rewards are an incentive. In the silent era, extras would happily hurl themselves off walls for the price of a few meals. Nowadays there are several dollar-millionaires in the stunting profession. The new breed approach the business more scientifically than their predecessors. One seasoned campaigner says of the youngsters: 'They have a mini-computer in one hand and a ready reckoner in the other!'

ANIMATION

Animation is the art of bringing drawings to life. It has been used by advertisers since the start of ITV because it has certain advantages. To begin with, it is very flexible. There is no limit to the number of styles a good studio can produce. The best animated commercials have great charm and tend to stay in the memory. They also appeal to everyone, whereas human performers, however popular, are bound to displease some viewers. Most important of all, there have been cases where sales of a product have doubled after campaigns featuring striking animation.

How it's done

Once an advertising agency has opted for the hand-made approach rather than live action, its creative staff work out their treatment in detail and take it to an animation studio. At this early stage the idea is set out on a storyboard, which is simply the plot explained in pictures. It looks something like a comic strip and can vary from crude sketches to finished designs. By using the storyboard, an artist can show others working on a production how the message is to be put across.

Next, a soundtrack is recorded, complete with music and dialogue. The animator listens over and over again to find out how long a word, a sound, or a single syllable lasts, so that the drawings can be made to measure. The track may also give some clues as to how a character should move.

Animators draw on sheets of paper slotted on to a peg bar to fix them in

At work in the studio on the 'Limara' commercial. Each cel is traced off over a light box.

The cels are then passed to two assistants who paint them in.
The cels are then spread on a table to dry.

The camera. On the bed is the final pack shot in 'Limara Body Fragrance' commercial.

position, and lit from underneath by a light box. Each drawing is very slightly different from the one before it. Flipping the sheets gives the illusion of movement. A minute of animated film can consist of anything up to 1 440 separate drawings.

After test-filming to see if any changes are needed, each sequence is tidied by assistants. They make sure the lines and shapes are clear and consistent.

Before they can be finally filmed, the drawings are traced with fine pens on to transparent acetate sheets called cels (cel is short for cellulose). These are then painted on the back with emulsion. Until cels were invented, backgrounds had to be laboriously copied on every sheet of paper. Now one cel can provide the setting for a whole sequence while others, bearing characters, are placed on top of it.

One last check and the cels are laid on a special table in the camera room and photographed, a frame at a time. Just as the drawings seemed to move when the sheets of paper were flipped, so later, when the film is projected at twenty-four frames per second, they will appear to have a life of their own.

Richard Williams at work in his office

Animation

Richard Williams

Richard Williams is one of the most
gifted animators in the business. As
a child of five in Canada, he saw the
Disney *Snow White* and never
looked back. For a while, when he
was starting out, he tried to make a
living as a painter but he found that
doing portraits for the wives of rich
industrialists was 'repulsive'. 'If
Rembrandt were alive today,' he
says 'he wouldn't be able to resist
animation.' Neither can Richard
Williams. He came to London and
after a lean period during which he
survived on a diet of peanut butter
and chips, he set up a successful
team.

His studio won an Oscar for its
animated version of *A Christmas
Carol* by Charles Dickens. It has
also been presented with literally
hundreds of awards for animated
commercials. Richard Williams has
drawn thousands of television
advertisements, not because he
particularly enjoys the work but in
order to raise money for his
magnificent dream.

Since the nineteen sixties he has

Williams' second-in-command with background drawings

been perfecting a full-length animated feature film which will run ninety minutes and promises to rival the finest achievements of Disney. The highly expensive project has had an uneven history of stops and starts but no one who has had so much as a glimpse of it can doubt its brilliance. It is a dazzling, imaginative, funny story set in the Middle East.

Richard Williams is grateful to television commercials for more than just money. They have taught him and his colleagues a great deal about technique. He feels that these short sprints have made them fit for the marathon. And 'marathon' is no exaggeration. On a top class full-length feature, an animator is doing well if he completes five minutes screen-time in a year. Roy Naisbitt, an associate director with Richard Williams, calculated that a single fiendishly complex sequence, in which a city seems to revolve as we approach it across the desert, could take him two years to draw.

Scheduling

Filling in the jigsaw

Every school plans its work round a timetable. The same goes for television companies. They call it a schedule.

The planners

To make life easier for themselves, programme planners, who are responsible for drawing up the schedules, divide the year into quarters. They then set about filling each thirteen-week period with the programmes they believe we will want to see.

The process begins many months earlier. The planners get together with controllers and heads of all production departments to discuss ideas and costings for the next financial year, which begins in April.

The pattern

By January, a pattern will start to emerge. The company will have decided to go ahead with certain projects and to shelve others. But still nothing is certain. Much depends on the availability of producers, artistes, studios and possibly Outside Broadcast units. If any piece of the jigsaw is missing, a whole series may have to be postponed or cancelled.

In the spring, a planner should know which major shows will be ready for the autumn quarter and can start to fill in some of the blank spaces on the schedule. For instance, a detective series may be placed for thirteen Fridays at eight o'clock, and a panel game on Wednesdays at seven.

Gradually, through the summer, the end of the year takes shape, although things can go wrong anywhere along the line. A leading actor may fall ill or pull out of a production for some other reason; a producer may not have the material ready in time, or a show might not be as good as it looked on paper.

The deadline

The absolute deadline for big decisions – the latest they can be made – is when the programme magazines 'go to press' (are prepared for printing). Information from the BBC has to reach *Radio Times* not later than ten days before it appears

on our bookstalls. If small changes are necessary after publication (for example when someone famous dies and a tribute displaces another programme) there is a danger that not all the viewers will know about the alterations.

The competition

Since BBC1 and ITV are in competition, planners on both sides are under added pressure to make their schedules as appealing as possible. If ITV fails to get a large audience it will have difficulty in persuading advertisers to buy time for their clients' products. On the other hand, if the BBC consistently falls too far behind, the Government will have an excuse not to give it extra money in the form of a bigger licence fee.

You could say that the schedulers for the two main channels have to go into battle blindfold. By the time they find out what the opposition has in mind, it will probably be too late to do anything about it. But even small pieces of information can be extremely useful.

The junction

ITV programmes tend to start exactly on the hour or the half-hour. The point is known as a 'junction'. This means that if a BBC planner can schedule a strong show to begin at ten minutes to the hour, the majority of the audience may be captured early and may be held for the rest of the evening.

In their turn, ITV planners know that the BBC mid-evening news will be at a fixed time, so that a blockbuster running against it might leave the BBC newsreader with relatively few viewers.

BBC2 and Channel Four do not need to compete in the same way. They were formed chiefly to cater for the people neglected by BBC1 and ITV. Each of them aims for about ten per cent of the audience. Occasionally when they show more popular items like comedy series, a successful film, or snooker they register a larger share.

The good planner

Good planners need a wide knowledge of broadcasting and an open mind about what the public wants to see. They should know how things were done in the past but be ready to try something new. Above all, they need an instinct for what will work and the patience to make it happen.

The twopenny wonder

'Height increased in thirty days. Five shillings for complete course. No appliances. No drugs. No dieting. The Melvin Strong system never fails.' So ran an intriguing advertisement in the first edition of *Radio Times* on 28 September 1923. Exactly how the unfailing Mr Strong managed to stretch his patients was not revealed. However, for twopence (astonishingly the price remained the same until 1952), the magazine also offered its readers, whether long, short, or tall, full details of 'wireless' programmes and a number of features; among them a piece by the Chief Engineer of the BBC called 'What are the wild waves saying?' and a reprinted talk on photographing animals by Major A. Ratclyffe Dugmore.

With the field to itself, the 'twopenny wonder' was an immediate success. By 1934, it was selling up to 2,000,000 copies a week. Ten years later the circulation had risen to 3,500,000; but the best was yet to come. The national obsession with radio after the War, followed by the triumphal television coverage of the Coronation in 1953, boosted sales to an incredible weekly average of 8,000,000 by the mid 1950s. Nowadays that figure is only reached (and overtaken) by the Christmas edition.

Radio Times counts its buyers anxiously because it must not make a loss. If that were to happen, we would be footing the bill with the money we pay for our television licence; a state of affairs which we would not tolerate. Fortunately the accounts of the magazine have always been healthily in the black and the enormous profits have been handed over to the BBC for programme making.

It probably seems strange to you that a publication should still be called *Radio Times* when the overwhelming majority of its readers are much more interested in television. The reason is that the title has become an institution. Who would dream of re-naming a great football club, like Arsenal, just because it sounds old-fashioned?

TVTimes

The debut of Independent Television in 1955 introduced a newcomer – *TVTimes* – to British bookstalls; and in subsequent years separate regional editions and some other ITV regional programme journals appeared, such as *TV Guide*, *Television Weekly*, *The Viewer*, and *Look Westward*. Understandably, sales of *Radio Times* were hit.

In 1968, the Independent Broadcasting Authority decided that ITV viewers would be better served by a single magazine, jointly owned by the ITV companies. Like *Radio Times*, *TVTimes* came into being to give more detailed information on programmes than can be found in the newspapers and to encourage the public to switch them on. Again like *Radio Times*, the magazine has in the process made large sums of money which have been handed back to the broadcasters for investment in production.

What's the difference?

So much for the similarities between the two publications. In spite of the fact that seventy per cent of the readership buy both, the editorial approaches and the presentation differ greatly.

Until its long overdue facelift, *Radio Times* was grey and uninviting. The efforts of its art editors and illustrators were often buried in a

Saturday: World of Sport

Shirley Crabtree, alias popular wrestler Big Daddy, is as soft out of the ring as he's hard inside it. The 23-stone giant, who can be seen in Saturday's *World of Sport*, explains to Ian Cotton how he switched from being wrestling's bad-guy to become a children's idol.

Why Big Daddy makes a huge splash with the children

continued on page 6

---

plain, earnest overall look. Now it is much better placed to compete for visual appeal with its ITV equivalent.

Compared with its BBC auntie, *TVTimes* is breezy, colourful and down to earth. The majority of its regular buyers are women and many of its features and advertisements naturally reflect the fact. Although the journal prides itself on being up to the minute, it is also frankly old-fashioned, with its fan-magazine faith in portraits of the stars (the editor of *Radio Times* wryly calls this the 'stars in their bathrooms' technique). That is not to say that there is no food for thought. An issue offering 'Brucie talking exclusively about life, love and the adorable new Mrs Forsyth' also carries a story about the Arab League, under the headline: 'Can democracy take root in the deserts?'

The cover of *TVTimes* is thought to have a tremendous effect on sales. The editor is under constant pressure from producers around the network, who may have spent months (and millions) on what they consider to be a masterpiece, to put their show on the front page. In the end, the image which will sell the most copies is usually the one which will be chosen. Here the creation of Channel Four proved to be a great bonus, since it brought to ITV a new, gutsy treatment of popular music for young people; a rich seam for *TVTimes* to mine.

Both programme magazines enjoy an average circulation between three and three and a half million, and both represent a considerable feat of organization. Each prints many different editions in several different centres, some of them hundreds of miles apart, using a combination of print systems. The material from all these sources has to be successfully 'married' and delivered via wholesalers and retailers to our doors.

Perhaps in decades to come, using already existing technology, we will be able to get our copy of *Radio Times* and *TVTimes* just by pressing a button on the television set and pulling the pages out of a convenient slot.

Job spot
The editorial team of *Radio Times* are all members of the BBC staff but the magazine does commission many articles from freelance journalists.

TVTimes has an editorial strength of one hundred and twenty people, including more than eighty journalists. The editor does not necessarily look for formal qualifications, preferring experience gained on newspapers or magazines, but membership of the National Union of Journalists is a must.

Blue Peter

The BBC has a much better record of programming for children than ITV. Some might say that it has had more practice, starting with radio, but that is not a very good excuse. The fact is simply that the Corporation has in general catered for its young viewers with more care and imagination than the commercial rivals.

Blue Peter is named after the blue and white flag raised within twenty-four hours of a ship leaving harbour. The show first went on the air in 1958. In 1971, it buried a box full of souvenirs, to be dug up by the presenters in the year 2000, so it obviously has no plans for early retirement.

4,000 letters a week
The secret of its unique success is involvement. Most television producers make programmes to suit their own tastes in the hope that they will also appeal to an audience. Blue Peter works the opposite way; seventy per cent of its ideas come from the viewers themselves. The comfortably cluttered office at the Television centre gets 4,000 letters a week – all of which, apart from competition entries, are eventually answered.

The production team feel that their most important job is to entertain. They believe, quite rightly, that you can be just as exhausted by a day at school as you might be after a shift on the docks. So why, when you get home, should you be faced with programmes which pompous adults think are 'good for you'?

The annual appeals
By taking an entertaining approach, Blue Peter has consistently attracted a large audience not only for lighthearted items, with the accent on do-it-yourself, but also for stories of great international importance. It regularly suggests practical ways of offering help.

The annual appeals, dating from 1962, have a habit of achieving far more than was ever expected. By asking for junk rather than money, the organizers make it possible for everyone to give equally.

One of the most overwhelming responses came in 1979. It was hoped

The Great
BLUE PETER
Bring & Buy Sale

that the Great *Blue Peter* Bring-and-Buy Sale would raise enough money to buy a lorry, 70 tons of rice, 42 tons of seed, 10,000 hoes and 1,000 fishing nets for the survivors of Pol Pot's murderous regime in Cambodia. In the event the total amounted to £3,710,823. It provided 57 lorries, thousands of tons of fertilizer, rice, and rice seed, 310,000 hoes, 1,000 doses of vaccine and 200 irrigation pumps. It also financed the hire of a DC 10 aircraft for eighteen days to airlift seed to Phnom Penh, and much more besides.

As well as encouraging concern and generous effort, the appeals widen young viewers' horizons. The *Blue Peter* Special Assignments, reporting from all over the world and on occasion recreating the lives of great men and women, have the same effect.

Biddy Baxter

Few programmes owe as much to a single personality as does *Blue Peter* to Biddy Baxter. From her arrival in 1962, she more than anyone else has given the show its sense of direction. Twenty years later she was presented with the Pye Award for Distinguished Services to Television. Under her editorship, the lively twice-weekly magazine has fostered not just regard for our fellow human beings but a fair deal for animals too. It has stressed that each needs the other by providing many guide dogs for the blind.

The *Blue Peter* pets

With the exception of a couple of unfortunate parrots, the *Blue Peter* menagerie have all become stars in their own right. There is something typically English about the fact that when you walk into the BBC Television Centre, you are confronted with a statue not of the founder but of a mongrel – Petra, *Blue Peter*'s first and best-loved pet.

Current affairs

Getting at the truth

You often hear the saying: 'It's a free country.' It is only partly true of course but certainly we have the freedom to ask questions about the way things are run. If we are not happy with the answers, we can and must say so. The trouble is that the people with power are hard to get at. In the course of our daily lives we do not bump into many Cabinet Ministers or industrial bosses. That is why it is vital to have strong and alert newspapers, radio and television (sometimes called 'the media'). They can ask the questions on our behalf and should go on asking them until they reach the truth. In many countries they are not allowed to do that. We are luckier than we realize.

Current affairs programmes, in particular, deal with matters of public importance. Their business is to investigate, reveal and, if necessary, criticize. The fact that they are in competition with each other – as well as with the press and radio – should make them all the more anxious to be sharp and efficient. There is little point in showing a story long after it has appeared in the headlines, unless fresh details have come to light.

How free is free?
This rather frightening picture is of a dead IRA hunger striker. His name was Patsy O'Hara. He starved himself to death because he wanted to draw the attention of the world to the demands of the IRA. The masked men surrounding the coffin are members of the same organization.

The photograph comes from a film made by *World in Action*. It was called *Ulster – The Propaganda War*. The programme set out to show how the IRA used events like the death of O'Hara to gain sympathy and support for its cause.

The Independent Broadcasting Authority said that unless the scene was taken out the programme could not be transmitted. Granada Television refused to make the cut and *Ulster – The Propaganda War* was therefore effectively banned. It has never been shown and neither has this picture.

The Independent Broadcasting Authority felt strongly that, if transmitted, the sequence might make matters worse in Northern Ireland. With the best of intentions, the Authority was acting as a censor.

We talked a moment ago about the saying: 'It's a free country.' But we have just seen that there are times when we are not free to say publicly what we believe to be true. Do you think that is a good thing or a bad thing?

World in Action
World in Action has been a leader in the field of international current affairs broadcasting for many years. With its familiar opening music, it is one of the mainstays of the ITV schedules.

Eighty per cent of its ideas come from members of the team. Most of the remainder are suggested by people who have at some time been associated with the programme. Subjects have to be weighty enough to fill half an hour and interesting enough to hold a large family audience. About a third of the stories

Alastair Burnett interviews Mrs Thatcher for TV Eye

are filmed abroad but these are not as popular as British-based coverage.

Like wildlife and news teams, current affairs units are no strangers to risk. A *World in Action* editor, Ray Fitzwalter, joked that the greatest danger he had faced was probably that of going blind in a public library while reading seventeen years of council minutes. The research was for a story about corruption. But he and his colleagues have, on occasions found themselves in frightening and explosive situations.

The year of the killing

There was the time when producer Mike Beckham and Fitzwalter were kidnapped in what is now Bangladesh. Their captors were the Mukhti Bahini guerrillas, fighting a civil war against the army of Pakistan. On their release, the *World in Action* unit were arrested yet again, this time by the army. They were ordered to give up half of their film because it was thought to show scenes which the military preferred to keep secret. Thinking fast, Beckham swapped the labels on the film-cans, handing over the less important half. He was

Job spot

When *World in Action* advertises a vacancy for a researcher, there can be as many as fifteen hundred replies. The programme does not think so much in terms of O and A level passes and university degrees. It is more interested in real intelligence, originality, and preferably some experience of radio, television or newspaper journalism. As well as being able to write, the perfect applicant would be part film-maker, accountant, lawyer, diplomat, doctor, psychologist, linguist, and mechanic. The ability to do without sleep for nights on end is an added bonus, together with a sense of humour. Needless to say, this ideal animal does not exist.

For the most part the new researcher will be involved not in revolutions or hunts for Nazi war criminals but in the day to day hard graft of checking, rechecking, knocking on doors, making endless telephone calls, querying company accounts, and generally forming patterns from fragments. It is tough, demanding work. The satisfaction lies simply in getting it right.

reluctant to lose even those but he had no option. Luckily informants later told him in which government office the footage was being stored and one of the guerrillas placed a limpet mine on the outside wall. After the explosion Beckham darted in, found the confiscated film and escaped through the back door, just as the Military police were coming in at the front.

At the airport Beckham boarded a plane, with the help of a forged VIP pass, but was promptly hauled off again by a confused army captain who said he had orders to stop him fleeing the country. Fortunately Beckham had a forged letter, with a later date, apparently giving him permission to leave. The film he and his colleagues brought back was called *The Year of the Killing*. As they watched it, the viewers had no idea of the risks involved in its making. Getting at the facts has cost other reporters their lives.

Take two

To help us understand exactly what happened, television sometimes reconstructs actual events. These pictures are from the restaging of an incident in London when police, on the track of a dangerous criminal, shot the wrong man by mistake.

Mastermind

Panel games and quizzes are popular with programme-makers because they are cheap to produce and relatively easy to organize. Viewers like them because at their best they combine drama, competition, knowledge, and sometimes, humour in a single, neat package.

Approaching menace

Mastermind, the most successful quiz of recent years, is a perfect example. The music (aptly called 'Approaching Menace'), the famous black chair, the dimmed lights, and the machine-gun style of questioning all help to create an atmosphere of tense expectation. As well as admiring the cleverness of the contestants and wondering which of them will win, we can have a go at beating them to the answers.

If the thought of actually taking part fills you with terror, it might not surprise you to know that the programme grew out of a nightmare. Bill Wright, who invented it, was shot down over Holland during the war and taken prisoner. He was suspected of being a spy and was interrogated. Many years later in 1971, by which time he was a BBC producer, the terrifying experience came back to him in a dream. When he woke up he realized that he had the perfect formula for a television inquisition.

Some four thousand people a year volunteer to show off their knowledge. After reading their applications the producer whittles the figure down to four hundred, who are then tested at a series of regional auditions. As a result, forty-eight are picked to do brain-battle for the *Mastermind* title and the trophy made of Caithness glass. To begin with, only a quarter of the final four dozen were women, but now the proportion is creeping closer to equality.

On the afternoon of programme day the contestants are put through a fairly lighthearted rehearsal, before facing their grilling in front of an audience.

The lonely figure

Although the quiz is recorded, once the lights go down and the chatter subsides, there is a keen sense of something exciting about to happen, with all eyes focused on the lonely figure in the middle. Keeping a cool head and determined concentration under such unnerving conditions must take considerable control. Most of us would probably be tempted to giggle.

The specialist questions are set by the leading authorities in the field concerned, many of them eminent academics. The General Knowledge rounds are compiled by a number of regular contributors. All the answers are thoroughly checked by a small team of researchers. If, during the recording, Magnus Magnusson is doubtful about a reply, the producer gives immediate guidance through an ear-piece.

The system is as fair as it can be. Great trouble is taken before taping to time the questions and ideal answers for each contestant so that no one has an advantage. In practice of course some react more slowly than others. The result is that fewer questions can be put to them in the period allowed. And General Knowledge is always bound to be partly a matter of luck.

In the warm-up, the producer stresses that *Mastermind* is only a game. In a way, strong though it is, the title is misleading. The players are not geniuses. They are ordinary men and women with a good grasp of some subjects, a lively interest in the world around them, a reliable memory and the ability to pluck facts from it instantly while under pressure.

Are you Mastermind material?

These General Knowledge questions have all been asked on the programme and are to be found, along with hundreds of others, in *Mastermind 4* published by the BBC. I am grateful to the producer for letting me reproduce them here.

1 What name is usually given to the poison contained in the plant Deadly Nightshade?
2 In geometry what is the name for a triangle in which only two sides are equal?
3 What is the name of the national park in California which contains the highest waterfall in North America?
4 The song 'I don't know how to love him' comes from which musical by Tim Rice and Andrew Lloyd Webber?
5 In a car engine what is the name of the branched pipe for distributing the air/fuel mixture to the cylinders?
6 What is the equivalent rank in the British Army of an Admiral of the Fleet?
7 In the human body what is the more common name for the sternum?
8 On 8 May each year the Furry

Dance takes place in Cornwall? Where?
9 In which classic adventure story do the characters of Dr Livesey and Squire Trelawney appear?
10 What is the motto of the Prince of Wales?
11 Which chemical element is named after a Greek word meaning colour?
12 In the poem 'Jabberwocky' in *Alice Through the Looking Glass* who or what were 'all mimsy'?
13 Which British city, other than London, has a main street called Piccadilly and a railway station called Victoria?
14 One of the wavebands on many ratio sets is labelled 'FM'. What does this stand for?
15 Who was the King at the time of the Gunpowder Plot?
16 A carnivorous animal eats flesh. What does a nucivorous animal eat?
17 The film *Chariots of Fire* is about two British Olympic Champions of the 1920's. Name one of them.
18 What is the offical language of Brazil?
19 According to the Old Testament,

the dove returned to Noah's Ark with a leaf. What kind of leaf?
20 In which ancient sport could you still compete in a York Round or a Hereford Round?

Answers
1 Belladonna (or Atropine)
2 Isosceles
3 Yosemite National Park
4 *Jesus Christ Superstar*
5 Induction or inlet or intake manifold
6 Field Marshal
7 Breastbone
8 Helston ('Furry' derives from the Latin *Feriae*: festivals, holidays)
9 *Treasure Island* by Robert Louis Stevenson
10 *Ich dien* (I Serve)
11 Chromium
12 The Borogroves
13 Manchester
14 Frequency Modulation
15 James I (and VI of Scotland)
16 Nuts
17 Harold Abrahams or Eric Liddell
18 Portuguese
19 Olive
20 Archery

Documentary

Television watching us

Picture a busy London street at lunchtime. Suddenly a car hurtles around the corner and screeches to a halt. Two masked men jump out, leaving a third at the wheel. The raiders smash the window of a Barclay's bank, lay a mattress over the jagged glass, and scramble in. Seconds later they re-emerge, carrying sacks which are evidently full of notes. The thieves have barely bundled themselves on to the back seat before the driver thumps the accelerator and makes a getaway.

The entire scene has been witnessed by a woman sitting in a parked car on the other side of the road. Throughout the action she has been calmly eating her sandwiches.

Afterwards she is asked whether she was alarmed by what she saw. 'No', she says. She 'thought they were making a film'.

What is real?

The point of the story, which actually happened, is that television has changed the way we look at events. It can tend to blur the line between what is real and what is invented.

Whether television is dealing with fact or fiction, it also has a habit of making things seem simpler and more dramatic than they are. The stars of detective series always get their man, often with a bullet in the head. The discussion in a current affairs programme usually features people with strongly opposed views; if they should nearly come to blows, so much the better.

Although most viewers watch in colour, many of the programmes they see present the world in terms of black and white. We know that in real life detectives do not always get their man. We know too that when it comes to complicated issues, like the debate over nuclear weapons, the majority are not posititively on one side or the other; they are not quite sure where they stand.

'I don't know'

This urge to over-simplify leads Roger Graef, one of our best documentary makers, to say the most interesting thing you can show on television is someone important admitting: 'I don't know.' Graef means the world is not clear cut. There are no easy answers, so why should we pretend there are? He believes that by putting stress on crisis and conflict, television has robbed our ordinary experiences of their dignity. It makes us feel that our own lives are less noteworthy and of less value than what we see on the small screen. Do you agree?

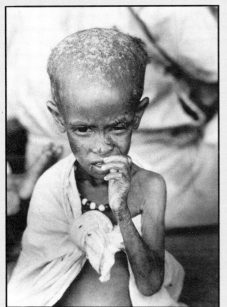

Pictures that shocked the world
There are times when television can really help. The agony of Ethiopia was literally brought home to us by a series of heartbreaking reports. As a result, relief agencies poured more aid into the country and a marathon televised concert in London and Philadelphia organised by Bob Geldof, raised over £50,000,000.

Ethiopia photos: Peter Dunne

John Grierson

The word 'documentary' was invented by a Scottish film maker, John Grierson. It is used to describe an approach which is neither news nor current affairs. A documentary deals with facts but in such a way that they are not out of date the day after we have seen them, as they are in a newspaper. Instead they will stay in our minds and tell us something important about ourselves and the world we live in. For example when Grierson made a film about fishermen, he did not simply tot up the number of herring they caught, as a news item might have done; he gave us an insight into the hardships, the disappointments, and the courage of the crews who bring home the catch from the North Sea. He created an impression which did not vanish overnight but which will always be relevant.

Police

Roger Graef works in the same tradition. *Police* took three years to complete. He shot it in Reading, which has one of the largest police stations in Europe. From the beginning, he intended to let the story tell itself. The characters would be seen crying, laughing, despairing, confessing, bullying, coaxing – just as they were at the time of filming. There was no commentary, no extra lighting, no attempt to stage-manage events.

Before filming started, the BBC team spent three months visiting Reading so that everyone would get used to them. Once they had picked the policemen, they virtually lived their lives with them for thirty weeks. We saw the police on raids, we saw them plotting, triumphant, downcast; we saw them and their suspects simply being human, like the rest of us. It was not a series of sensational highlights,

of stark blacks and whites; like our own existence, it was mostly grey.

But Graef thought the Reading police enjoyed talking about their deeds more than doing them. He felt they went on more raids than were necessary, just because they were exciting, and that the impossible example set by television cops was chiefly to blame. As a result, he believes, the lonely dedication of the constable pounding the beat is less valued than it was.

But if the small screen has its drawbacks, it has its strengths too. No matter what the subject, all good documentaries turn the tables; they are television watching us. We ought to be able to learn something.

Comedy

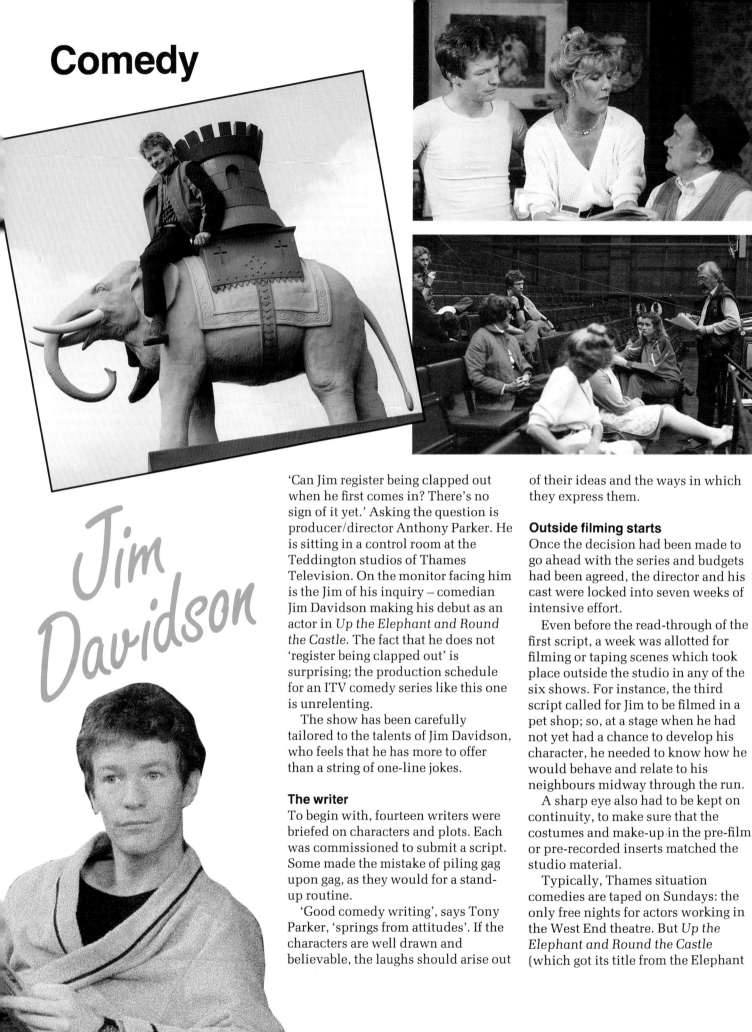

Jim Davidson

'Can Jim register being clapped out when he first comes in? There's no sign of it yet.' Asking the question is producer/director Anthony Parker. He is sitting in a control room at the Teddington studios of Thames Television. On the monitor facing him is the Jim of his inquiry – comedian Jim Davidson making his debut as an actor in *Up the Elephant and Round the Castle*. The fact that he does not 'register being clapped out' is surprising; the production schedule for an ITV comedy series like this one is unrelenting.

The show has been carefully tailored to the talents of Jim Davidson, who feels that he has more to offer than a string of one-line jokes.

The writer

To begin with, fourteen writers were briefed on characters and plots. Each was commissioned to submit a script. Some made the mistake of piling gag upon gag, as they would for a stand-up routine.

'Good comedy writing', says Tony Parker, 'springs from attitudes'. If the characters are well drawn and believable, the laughs should arise out of their ideas and the ways in which they express them.

Outside filming starts

Once the decision had been made to go ahead with the series and budgets had been agreed, the director and his cast were locked into seven weeks of intensive effort.

Even before the read-through of the first script, a week was allotted for filming or taping scenes which took place outside the studio in any of the six shows. For instance, the third script called for Jim to be filmed in a pet shop; so, at a stage when he had not yet had a chance to develop his character, he needed to know how he would behave and relate to his neighbours midway through the run.

A sharp eye also had to be kept on continuity, to make sure that the costumes and make-up in the pre-film or pre-recorded inserts matched the studio material.

Typically, Thames situation comedies are taped on Sundays: the only free nights for actors working in the West End theatre. But *Up the Elephant and Round the Castle* (which got its title from the Elephant and Castle area of London) varied the pattern. We will follow its progress in the lead-up to a Tuesday recording.

Rehearsals

The read-through was held on a Thursday. Next came two more days in a rehearsal room where, with the measurements of the eventual set marked out on the floor, the cast ran through lines and actions while the director decided exactly how he would deploy his five cameras.

On Sunday, the writer was invited to see what had been made of the dialogue. The following day, cameramen and sound engineers joined the team. By now complete camera scripts had been handed out, giving details of anything up to 250 shots with which the director planned to tell the story. Since the overall running time (minus beginning and end credits) was twenty-three minutes, that meant a change of shot on average every five and a half seconds.

Into the studio

On Tuesday the production moved into the studio, where the morning was taken up with a painstaking rehearsal of camera positions. After lunch there was another run-through before the dress rehearsal. This was the last opportunity for the director to correct mistakes. Throughout it he would keep up a commentary of observations, noted by the production assistant, cameras, sound, and the floor manager: 'There's a bit of shadowing there – talk to lighting. . . Watch the head moving on that – I don't like it disappearing out of the top of frame. . . .'

At six-thirty in the evening, the director gave the cast their last instructions, quietly pointing out where improvements could still be made and building confidence with praise.

The performance

The hard work of six days was about to reach its climax. A warm-up man got the audience in the right mood, skilfully putting them at their ease in a strange environment. His humour

had to be funny enough to relax them but not so hilarious that it made the show look lame by comparison.

By eight-thirty the rows of expectant faces helped the cast to feel a sense of occasion, just as they would in the theatre. The adrenalin began to focus their concentration. The hours in bare rehearsal rooms, the learning, the repetition, and the waiting were about to pay off. The production assistant counted down to zero. The titles rolled. The audience was attentive. Jim, now looking suitably 'clapped out', began his long opening speech.

For the actors who were not involved in other shows, Wednesday was a day off. The director would probably spend it in an editing suite. For everyone, the ball started to roll again on Thursday, with a new script and a fast approaching deadline.

The News from

ITN 1

The spider and the web

Is the news boring?

In our middle school years, many of us tend to find the news boring. It seems to grind on endlessly about strikes, speeches, rising prices, and wars in far-away countries with difficult names. As we grow older, we take more interest; eventually we may feel out of touch if we have not heard or seen at least one bulletin during the day.

The story of how the news is gathered and broadcast is far from boring. In its way, it is the most exciting work in television. The people involved have to be ready to react instantly to events of major importance happening anywhere in the world at any hour of the twenty-four. News never rests and can never be taken for granted. It calls for alertness and good judgement (sometimes called 'a nose'; that is the ability to take in a few sparse facts and to have a hunch that they are simply the tip of a fascinating iceberg).

ITN

ITN (Independent Television News) belongs to the ITV companies and gives them three bulletins every weekday: *News at One*, *News at 5.45* and, most famously, *News at Ten*. There are three shorter bulletins on Saturdays and two on Sundays: ITN also provides *Channel Four News*, as well as supplying news pages for the ITV teletext service, Oracle, and 'specials' on big occasions like General Elections and Royal Tours.

The Task Force landing in the Falklands

ITN headquarters, not far from Oxford Circus in London, is the spider at the centre of a vast web. News stories happen at the outermost strands of the web and are fed through to the ever-hungry spider in a variety of ways – on telephone and teleprinter lines, via satellite and aboard aircraft. Constantly shuttling backwards and forwards along the intersecting threads is an urgent stream of editors, reporters and camera crews.

A helicopter under fire in the Falklands

'Jet-crash in Italy'

There is no such thing as a typical news story, but let us suppose that a jumbo jet has crashed in northern Italy. Through the first people on the scene (possibly farmers, fishermen, or police) the information will very soon reach a local reporter or news agency. The Italian state television service, RAI, will be alerted and the pictures it shoots will be offered internationally. (Eurovision gives broadcasters in Europe and elsewhere access to a common pool of material by linking

them together three times a day and showing them what is available.)

Meanwhile the ITN foreign desk will be up with the story and may well decide to use the Eurovision source for the first bulletin but to send their own reporter and camera team for a more detailed treatment of the disaster.

On the road

Within minutes of getting the message, the ITN crew will be on the

The right to work demonstration by members of the Nottingham branch of the National Union of Mineworkers

road, heading for the nearest airport to catch either a scheduled flight or a specially chartered plane.

As soon as they arrive at the site of the crash they will set about piecing together the facts, interviewing rescuers and survivors, trying to pinpoint the cause. They must work thoroughly but fast; in our system it is not enough to report the news

Eyeball to eyeball on the miners' picket-line at Tow Law in County Durham

A policeman watches over the badly damaged Grand Hotel in Brighton after the IRA bomb blast on 12 October 1984

accurately – it is also important to do so before the opposition can get a look in.

For many years, stories like this could only be covered on film. It was then a matter of arranging to get the footage back to London, (using any means of transport including motorcycles, cars and planes) having it processed at a laboratory, cutting

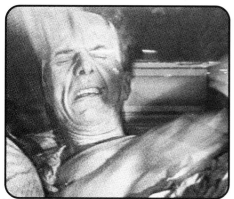

Norman Tebbit, the Industry Secretary, being cut free after the Brighton bomb explosion

out what was not wanted with a razor blade, and joining the rest together with special tape. You can imagine how much precious time was wasted.

ENG

The breakthrough came with ENG (Electronic Newsgathering). It uses a small television camera attached to a lightweight videotape recorder. The pictures, with sound, can be beamed directly back to headquarters, with the help of a links vehicle and/or a

satellite, and can be electronically edited at the press of several buttons.

In some companies there was resistance to ENG from trade unions who felt that it could lead to fewer jobs for their members.

Input and output

The raw material of ITN news programmes, like the Italian story whose progress we have been following, is known as 'input'. As soon as an item reaches base, it comes

The State Opening of Parliament

under the charge of the 'output' or production team who will screen it.

When the plane crash coverage has been viewed, a scriptwriter will be assigned to supervise the editing of the story and to write whatever additional commentary, links, and introduction may be necessary. At ITN, on some items newscasters do their own writing.

The programme editor, who decides what will be included in a bulletin,

The funeral of Indira Gandhi

Damage in the streets of Northern Ireland

will already have judged the value or 'weight' of the Italian report and will have given it a place in the running-order. Later events might make it even stronger, possibly promoting it to 'lead story'. We will see more of that process in the next chapter.

The plane crash example is one tiny part of one broadcast on one day. Round the clock at ITN, tips and stories are flooding in from contacts, journalists, press officers, national and international news agencies, ITV newsrooms, Eurovision, the House of Commons (where all big speeches and debated are recorded), and other sources. This mass of information has to be sifted and checked before crews can be sent out to turn it into pictures.

The News from

ITN₂

Countdown: day

Every weekday at ITN, different teams working shift systems gear themselves up to a series of highpoints – *News at One*, *News at 5.45*, *Channel Four News*, and *News at Ten*. As we have seen, each bulletin is made up of material from a worldwide network of sources and yet each has its own distinct character.

The ITN flagship is *News at Ten*. Here are just a few moments from its timetable on an average day – a day which has no clear beginning or end, because news is no respecter of clocks, but which reaches a climax with the familiar bongs of Big Ben.

7.30 am News editors arrive at ITN headquarters in Wells Street, after listening to the radio news and reading the newspapers. For the next three hours they review plans made yesterday and decide how to handle the stories which they believe should be covered today.

10.30am Morning meeting
The overall editor of ITN, or a deputy, will preside. Also present are the news and foreign editors of the day, as well as the programme editors of each bulletin and the people responsible for assigning crews and technical facilities. By the end of the meeting, agreement will have been reached on the main stories to be tackled. Crews speed off to cover them.

11.45 Two new stories break and room is made for them. The output team are discussing how the various items should be presented on the screen, ordering maps, graphs and other illustrations from graphics.

Meanwhile copytasters are sampling the continuous flow of teleprinter wordage from agencies and passing it on to those who need it.

Scriptwriters may be researching background details with the help of cuttings, reference books, and files in the News Information library on the premises. Videotape is viewed and edited in a dozen suites. Still photographs and videotape or film are selected for back-up from the carefully catalogued ITN reference libraries. And what seem like a thousand telephones ring in relays.

This is the pattern during the next few hours, during which other bulletins generate other meetings and lunch may or may not be taken.

1pm The first ITN bulletin of the day. The *News at 5.45*, *Channel Four News*, and *News at Ten* production teams take note of the content and the way in which it is presented.

3.45pm Look-ahead meeting
As its name implies, this is a chance to see what the following day is likely to bring, for instance, a major speech by a leading politician or a colourful royal occasion. In the event, these stories may be forced out by more pressing news but they have to be planned for.

5pm The *News at Ten* team, including newscasters, hear how things stand from the programme editor. The shape of the bulletin is beginning to emerge but late stories may call for big changes. It is still only mid-day in New York, for instance, and a trans-Atlantic telephone call or an urgent agency report can mean a complete re-think.

5.45pm News at 5.45

Here is an actual running-order for this bulletin. See how it compares with the lead stories in *News at Ten* later on:

1 Ex-police chief defends selling memoirs of murder case to a newspaper.
2 Price of petrol goes up.
3 British scientists claim breakthrough in cancer research.
4 American number one seed through to mens' singles final at Wimbledon.
5 Murder hunt in Derbyshire.
6 Youth to be detained in mental hospital for killing twelve-year-old boy.
7 Londonderry woman dies protecting husband from IRA gunmen.
8 PLO sends delegation to Syria.
9 Former Speaker of House of Commons made Viscount.
10 Birthday of Princess Diana in Canada.

What do *you* think?

It is interesting to note that half of the stories in this edition are about violent death or disease. This is not a sign of ghoulishness but a reflection of the balance of news on a particular day. In any case, the cancer story is about hope rather than despair. But all bulletins are merely selections and it may be that our appetite for sensation means that acts of violence are sometimes selected in preference to more significant but less gory items. What do *you* think?

The News from ITN 3

Countdown: night

7pm The main meeting for *News at Ten*

It is short and informal. The entire output team, including newscasters, studio director, chief sub-editor, vision mixer, scriptwriters, and people in charge of technical facilities perch on desks in the newsroom, surrounded by small television sets, scripts, newspapers, and telephones.

The programme editor has decided that the cancer story should be promoted to the lead. The memoirs of the ex-police chief will drop to second and third will come the Derbyshire murders – 'we'll take a map on that one.' The report on the petrol price-rise, seen at 5.45, needs to be re-edited 'if we use it at all and I'm very sceptical on that.' Many more items, including marvellous pictures of an erupting volcano, are discussed at what seems like dizzy speed. The point is that by now everyone present knows the details and there is no need to spell them out. The crisp conversation is conducted in a sort of oral shorthand.

Finally a decision is made about the 'bongs', the ITN name for the punchy headlines of *News at Ten* delivered between the chimes of Big Ben. Tonight they will feature the following stories: cancer, petrol, Wimbledon, Royals, and volcano.

Although the content of the bulletin is now becoming clearer, it is by no means set in concrete. The programme editor is prepared to throw anything overboard if an important story breaks before ten o'clock. In the meantime, all the material needed to illustrate twenty items is prepared and the remaining scripts are written by scriptwriters and newscasters. Once they have been checked by the chief sub-editor and the programme editor, they can be typed on 'greys' – the copies on grey paper actually used in the studio.

9.32pm In the studio control room, facing fifty monitor screens, the vision mixer practises some of the effects to be used in the programme, such as dividing the screen into four squares, each of which can show a different picture.

9.40 The newscasters arrive in the studio for a short rehearsal. They are still re-writing scripts.

9.48 The director says: 'Let's start by rehearsing the bongs. We haven't got the pictures for the last two yet.' There is a feeling of tension in the control room, with a number of reports and illustrations still in preparation.

9.57 Another rehearsal of the bongs, this time with the two missing visuals.

9.58 A voice over the talkback (the link between the studio and the control room) says: 'There's still a problem in graphics; they say I'm wasting my time talking to them because they're not ready.'

9.59 The director gets on the internal telephone to graphics: 'We need those graphics in one minute.'

9.59¾ 15 seconds to go. A voice from the studio floor over talkback: 'The graphics have just come in.'
Hardly time for a sigh of relief before:

10pm The familiar music; planet Earth, the Telecom Tower, Big Ben, the bongs – one of the most intricate sequences in television using pictures from half a dozen sources in twenty-five seconds. *News at Ten* is off to a confident start, creating order out of what looks to the observer like chaos. The first half goes like this:
  1 Cancer breakthrough.
  2 Memoirs of ex-police chief.
  3 Derbyshire murders.
  4 Petrol price rise.

10.06 The programme editor passes late information to the senior newscaster via his ear-piece. (The newscasters use a teleprompter which reflects the words over the lens of the camera but for last-minute changes they may have to rely on their scripts.)
  5 Environment Minister says that under its present leadership 'the Greater London Council is not so much a Town Hall as a Music Hall.' The wrong name is superimposed on the screen. 'Oh, sherbet,' says the programme editor. The production team, who want their work to look perfect, are sharply disappointed.
  6 Former Speaker of House of Commons made Viscount.
  7 Northern Ireland Minister condemns remarks made by UDA.
  8 American Number One to play unseeded opponent in Wimbledon's mens' final.

10.13 Preview of what is to come in Part Two.

10.14 Commercial break.

During the break, the programme editor passes instructions about cuts and additions to the newscasters. Still surviving from the *News at 5.45*, the stories about the PLO and the woman who shielded her husband from the bullets of the IRA share the second half with, among other items, a scandal in Washington, a dam in Tasmania, the future of Hong Kong, a volcano in Hawaii, job gains and losses, and the youngest athlete ever to run for England. The birthday of Princess Diana ends the bulletin on a happy note. The newscasters turn to chat to each other, unheard by us, and another *News at Ten* instantly belongs to the past tense; at once the focus shifts to tomorrow.

How would you do it?
Try watching a bulletin carefully. Make a note of the items and see if you agree with the order in which they are shown. You might think that the first story is not as important as one of the others. If there is a report showing two points of view, see whether they have both been treated fairly. Has an item been included not because it has something to say but simply because it is exciting to look at? Decide how you might have done things differently.

Will it rain tomorrow?

Jack Scott giving us the bad news

Weather forecast

Talking about the weather

We British are not the only people who talk about the weather all the time; most nations with changeable climates are just the same.

Here, as elsewhere, it is obviously vitally important for groups such as fliers, sailors, farmers, and organizers of sporting events to know what to expect, so that they can adjust their activities accordingly.

For the rest of us, weather is largely a matter of whether: whether to chance a trip to the seaside or even whether to risk hanging out the washing. But although we have less at stake than those whose livelihood depends on accurate forecasting, you would never think so to hear us earnestly discussing temperatures and trends.

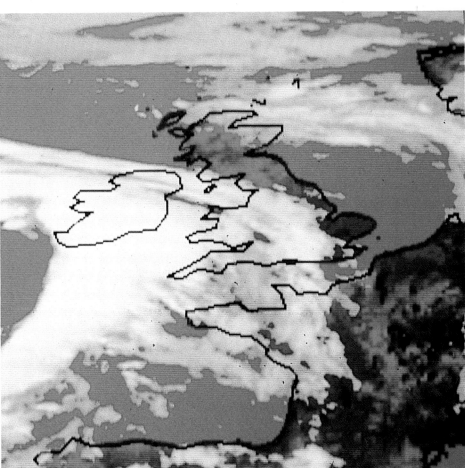

Computer-generated weather map of the British Isles and Western Europe, showing the passing of a depression

Snish

Styles of television forecasting vary. In this country forecasters use a straightforward approach. In the United States some of them perform with great gusto, using their arms like semaphore flags and inventing a whole new vocabulary to get their message across. One of them for instance coined the word 'snish' for snow showers.

Regardless of how they choose to present what they have to say, all forecasters rely on a system which dates back to 1873. In that year, what is now called the World Meteorological Organization came into being. Since then, except in times of war, all the member countries have freely exchanged information on the weather. They now do so on an hourly basis, collecting data from thousands of weather stations (both manned and unmanned) and sending it out in the form of an international figure code.

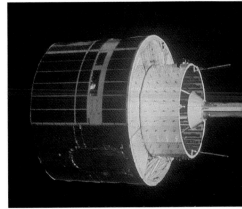

A meteosat (weather satellite)

Computers to the rescue

In 1921, a British scientist calculated that it would take 64,000 mathematicians working flat out to keep abreast of what the weather was doing at any given moment, let alone what it would look like in an hour or two. Fortunately computers came to the rescue. When it was installed in 1981, the main computer at the Bracknell headquarters of the United Kingdom Meteorological Office was the most powerful in the world. Although its 'brain' is only the size of half a dozen wardrobes, it can do 400,000,000 sums per second.

When it has digested the almost unimaginable mass of information fed into it from all over the globe, the Bracknell computer passes on its findings to another labour-saving device which reproduces them in the form of a chart – the sort we see on television. Forecasting stations, like the London Weather Centre (and the BBC itself) can then get exact copies of the chart from machines in their own offices.

Isobars and fronts

The next step is to draw on isobars and fronts, showing patterns of wind and rain. With a chart for midday, another for 3pm, another for 6pm and so on, it is literally possible to flick the set and to see how things are moving. The skill of forecasting lies in completing the next chart in the series; the one predicting the future rather than recording the past.

If there were weather stations placed a few miles apart over the entire face of the earth, forecasts would be near enough one hundred per cent accurate. We would have so much knowledge that we could be certain of trends. But most of the planet is covered by water; there is an ice-cap at each Pole and the poorer countries of what we call the Third World cannot afford the facilities.

These gaps represent an unknown factor for forecasters. It is a bit like being asked: 'what is the total of 2+2+?'

Satellites

With the introduction of satellites, the science has advanced dramatically. We can now see pictures of the places which are not supplying information, complete with cloud formations. Satellites also help us to gauge pressure, wind-speed, and relative humidity so that we can plot the state of the atmosphere. And where once we had to send up brave scientists, equipped with thermometers, in hot air balloons to measure temperature changes as they went aloft, we now have expensive hardware to do the job for us.

Backed up by developing technology, television weather forecasters have to tailor their predictions to suit their audience. The millions of us who watch, hoping for the best, are not experts. We want to hear the answers to what we think are simple questions. Will it rain tonight? Will it be as hot tomorrow as it was today? All the complex facts from a vast network must be reduced to language we can easily understand.

The future

Eventually it will probably be possible to foretell the weather months ahead. That may be a happy prospect for farmers but it will burden

The London Weather Centre

the television meteorologists themselves with an awful responsibility. Let us suppose that they reveal in March that the summer is going to be a washout. The seaside landladies of Britain would set up lynching parties to strangle the forecasters with their own isobars. Perhaps the poet Thomas Gray was right: 'Where ignorance is bliss', he wrote, ''tis folly to be wise.'

Night Beat News (Sianel Pedwar Cymru). Looks like rain again

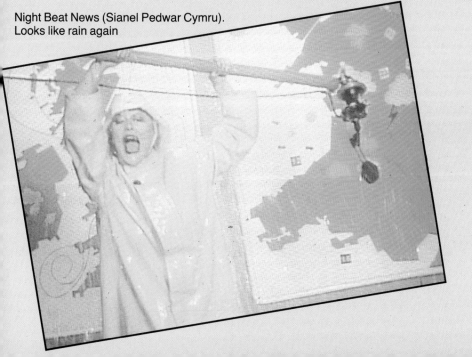

Transmission control

Putting the programme on the air

The daily output of any television company is obviously made up of a wide variety of programmes. It may include broadcasts for schools, entertainment for the under-fives, shows for women, sport, news, a slot in the afternoon for children, an evening magazine, a soap opera, comedy, documentary, drama, discussion, a feature film, and so on.

The transmission controller
Some shows will be live, others recorded. Of those already made, most will be on videotape, the remainder on film. Deciding where each should fit into the overall pattern is, as we have seen, the job of the planners; actually putting the programmes on the air is the business of the transmission controller.

The schedule from which the transmission controller works is a precise document. From the moment when the station opens in the morning until close-down, every single second is accounted for. This is particularly important in ITV where time sold to advertisers pays the wages.

As well as telling the transmission controller how long a show should run, when it is due to start and end, and the exact points at which the commercial breaks are to be inserted, the schedule reveals the source of the programme. Staying with ITV, because it consists of fifteen distinct companies and is therefore more complex than the BBC, the material might have come:
1) from the station which is transmitting it, either live or recorded;
2) live or recorded from one of the other fourteen stations (ITN – the news station - is a further source);
3) from a foreign company, probably pre-packaged but possibly via satellite.

The announcer
At a glance then, the team headed by the transmission controller knows what is coming, when, and where from. To make the job even harder, they are also responsible for the announcers, working on a rota system from a small presentation studio.

Whether in or out of vision, the announcers need to be skilled professionals. They work long shifts with one eye constantly on the clock. It is largely up to them to express the personality (sometimes called the 'house-style') of a station. They provide an up-to-the-minute information service, reminding viewers of what is in store, detailing changes, and occasionally reading dramatic news flashes.

But it is in cases of real emergency that announcers are invaluable. If for any reason a programme underruns or is interrupted by a technical failure, the transmission controller will simply telephone the presentation studio and the experienced announcer will coolly fill what could otherwise be an embarrassing pause.

Talking your way out
There are some crises, though, which cannot be entirely talked away. A senior transmission controller in ITV recalls a day when the highlight of the afternoon was to be eighty minutes of horse racing from York. The station announcer set the scene and handed over to the course, where the commentator welcomed viewers. Since the first commercial break was not due for twenty minutes or so, the transmission controller lowered the sound and settled down with a cup of tea. Two minutes later, to his horror, he dimly heard the commentator

The transmission controller

A loggist

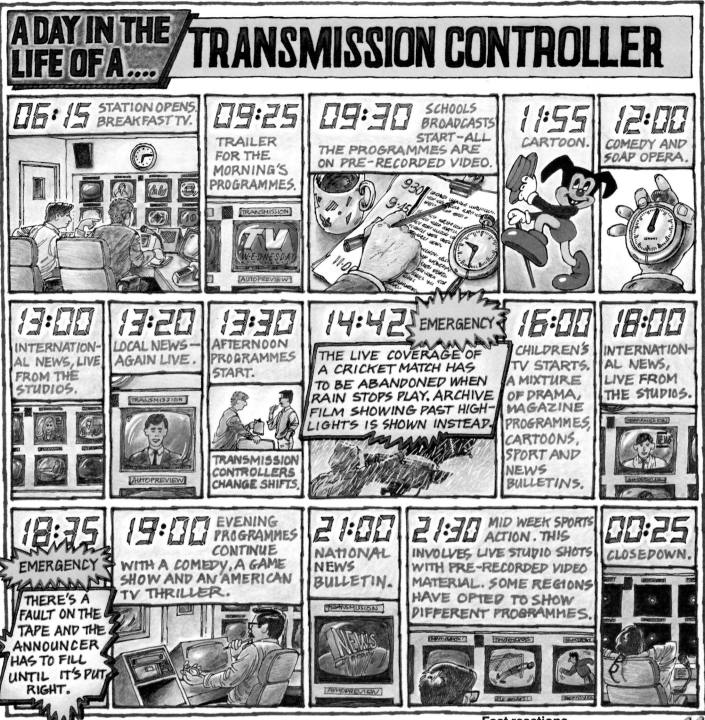

Fast reactions

saying that weather conditions at York had rapidly gone from bad to worse and that the stewards had decided to abandon the meeting. With that, the racing correspondent raised his hat and bade his bewildered public 'good afternoon'.

On the red telephone which links the central control rooms of all the companies in the ITV network, the transmission controller, still choking on his tea, was informed by Yorkshire Television, who had been covering the event, that he was now on his own for the next seventy-eight minutes. Making a quick recovery, he asked his valiant announcer to fill while a standby feature film was prepared for screening.

Happenings of international importance, like the sudden resignation or death of a Head of State call for fast reactions over a long period; perhaps even for the reorganization of an entire schedule as it unfolds.

In a sense, transmission controllers add the final polish to the programmes we see; their aim is to make the flow look smooth and effortless.

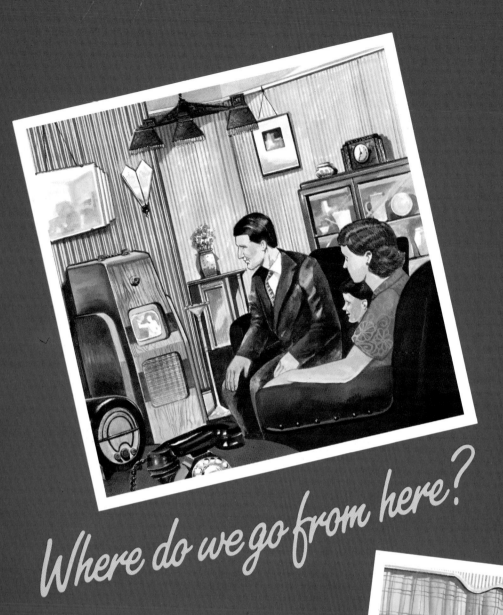

Does that make us want to imitate what we see? When a favourite detective shoots a crook, do you feel like going out and gunning down a neighbour? Some experts think that seeing too much casual violence does tend to make us more aggressive. Others believe that we are well able to tell the difference between fantasy and reality, and to keep the two in separate compartments.

But there is another worrying possibility. Could it be that because we do see so many brutal beatings and murders, we may begin to take them for granted? and eventually care less about the way we treat each other?

Does television make us lazy?

At a more everyday level, there is concern that television makes us lazy. After watching for hours on end without having to make any effort, we may start to enjoy not using our mind. The result may be that what one researcher has called the 'drug' of constant, undemanding entertainment will turn us into adults who dislike work of any kind (always assuming that there is any for us to do) and who are often bored.

Where do we go from here?

Do we imitate what we see?

No so long ago it was suggested that, like cigarette packets, some television programmes should carry a government health warning. The idea sounds ridiculous but it came up in a sensible, televised discussion about violence on the screen.

A researcher in the United States has claimed that by the time the average American viewer reaches the late teens, he or she will have witnessed some 18,000 violent deaths in fictional shows.

In the case of the British viewer, the figure may be lower; but the fact remains that if we are raised in a home with a television set, we are likely to see a great deal of blood spilled by characters who seem to think no more of killing than of blowing their nose.

thirty or forty channels is only exciting if they have something worthwhile to offer; and if they do not further divide the nation. We must see to it that viewers do not lose out on an excellent, complete service just because they cannot afford the glamorous extras made available by the new technology.

It depends on you

You have an important say in where we go from here, whether you decide to work in television, or whether you just make sure that your views are heard. The broadcasters will ignore you at their peril. When you are old enough to pay for a television licence, you are immediately a shareholder in the BBC. It is your money they are spending. On all channels you can use your vote by switching off or by writing to suggest or complain. Do not be afraid to go straight to the top, if necessary addressing your letter to the managing director or even the chairman.

It is no good sitting in an armchair and moaning that television is rubbish; make it better.

Will we get it right?

We need to give these matters some careful thought as we move into a new television era. The remaining years of the century are likely to see a broadcasting explosion. Satellite channels are only the beginning. We have already looked at the strides made by teletext and, despite not very encouraging experiments , cable services widen our choice considerably. Add the expanding production of video cassettes and you have as wide a field of vision as anyone could want.

So far in British television, we have managed to get it right. BBC1 and BBC2, and ITV offer a good balance of programming. Channel Four has successfully filled a large gap by letting independent producers make programmes which do not necessarily have to attract enormous ratings. It has also helped the ailing British film industry.

Making sure that we get the next step right too has been causing a great many headaches. The prospect of

Further information

BBC

Head Office
Broadcasting House
Portland Street
London W1A 4WW
Tel: 01-580 4468

BBC Television Centre
Wood Lane
London W12 7RJ
Tel: 01-743 8000

BBC Ticket Unit
BBC London W1A 4WW
Tel: 01-580 4468

Top of the Pops Ticket Unit
BBC Television Centre
Wood Lane
London W12 7RJ
Tel: 01-743 8000

Birmingham
British Broadcasting Centre
Pebble Mill Road
BIRMINGHAM B5 7SA
Tel: 021-472 5353

Bristol
Bristol Broadcasting House
Whitelady's Road
BRISTOL BSA 2LR
Tel: 0272 32211

Norwich
BBC
Saint Catherine's Close
All Saints Green
NORWICH
Norfolk NR1 3ND
Tel: 0603 28841

Manchester
PO BOX 27
New Broadcasting House
Oxford Road
MANCHESTER M60 1SJ
Tel: 061-236 8444

Leeds
Broadcasting Centre
Woodhouse Lane
LEEDS LS2 9PX
Tel: 0532 441188

Southampton
South Weston House
Canute Road
SOUTHAMPTON SO9 1PF
Tel: 0703 26201

Northern Ireland
Broadcasting House
25–27 Ormeau Avenue
BELFAST BT2 8HQ
Tel: 0232 44400

Glasgow
Broadcasting House
Queen Margaret Drive
GLASGOW G12 8DG
Tel: 041 339 8844

Wales
Cardiff Broadcasting House
Llantrisant Road
Llandaff
CARDIFF CF5 2YO
Tel: 0222 564888

IBA

Headquarters
70 Brompton Road
London SW3 1EY
Tel: 01-584 7011

ITV

Anglia Television
Anglia House
NORWICH NR1 3JG
Tel: 0603 615151

Border Television
Television Centre
CARLISLE CA1 3NT
Tel: 0228 25101

Central Independent Television
Central House
Broad Street
BIRMINGHAM B1 2JP
Tel: 021-643 9898

Newland House
Mount Street
NOTTINGHAM NG1 6GN
Tel: 0602 413111

Channel Television
The Television Centre
St Helier
Jersey
CHANNEL ISLANDS
Tel: Jersey (0534) 73999

Grampian Television
Queen's Cross
ABERDEEN AB9 2XJ
Tel: 0224 53553

Granada Television
Granada TV Centre
MANCHESTER M60 9EA
Tel: 061-832 7211

HTV Wales
Television Centre
CARDIFF CF1 9XL
Tel: 0222 21021

HTV West
Television Centre
Bath Road
BRISTOL BS4 3HG
Tel: 0272 778366

London Weekend Television
South Bank Television Centre
Kent House
Upper Ground
LONDON SE1 9LT
Tel: 01-261 3434

Scottish Television
Cowcaddens
GLASGOW G2 3PR
Tel: 041 332 9999

Television South West
Derry's Cross
PLYMOUTH PL1 2SP
Tel: 0752 663322

Thames Television
Thames Television House
306–316 Euston Road
LONDON NW1 3BB
Tel: 01-387 9494

TVS (Television South)
Television Centre
Northam Road
SOUTHAMPTON SO9 5HZ
Tel: 0703 34211

Kent House
Lower Stone Street
MAIDSTONE ME15 6NT
Tel: 0622 54945

Tyne Tees Television
The Television Centre
City Road
NEWCASTLE UPON TYNE NE1 2AL
Tel: 0632 610181

Ulster Television
Havelock House
Ormeau Road
BELFAST BT7 1EB
Tel: 0232 28122

Yorkshire Television
The Television Centre
LEEDS LS3 1JS
Tel: 0532 438283

Independent Television News
ITN House
48 Wells Street
LONDON W10 4DE
Tel: 01-637 2424

Independent Television Companies Association
Knighton House
56 Mortimer Street
LONDON W1N 8AN
Tel: 01-636 6866

Independent Television Publications Ltd
247 Tottenham Court Road
LONDON W1P 0AU
Tel: 01-636 3666

Oracle Teletext Ltd
Craven House
25–32 Marshall Street
LONDON W1V 1LL
Tel: 01-434 3121

Channel Four

Channel Four Television Company Ltd
60 Charlotte Street
LONDON W1P 2AX
Tel: 01-631 4444

Sianel Pedwar Cymru (S4C)
Clos Sophia
CAERDYDD (CARDIFF) CF1 9XY
Tel: 0222 43421)

The Video Box
Charlotte Street
London W1
Tel: 01-631 4444

Breakfast TV

TV-AM
Breakfast Television Centre
Hawley Crescent
LONDON NW1 8EF
Tel: 01-267 5483

Index

Acknowledgements

I would like to thank the following for their help:

Biddy Baxter; Roy Bottomley; Tom Brennand; John Brown; Peter Day; Michael De Salis; Frank Dewsbury; Leita Don; Mike Fentiman; David Filkin; Brian Gearing; Roger Graef; Leslie Halliwell; Michaeljohn Harris; Ashley Hill; Michael Hurll; Julie Jackson; David Klein; Bonnie Langford; Roy Lomas; Roger Mackay; David Mannion; Maggie McPherson; Malcolm Morris; John Nathan-Turner; Anthony Parker; Anthony Peagam; Jim Pople; Joan Riley; Ann Rosenberg; Robert Rowland; Peggy Saunders; Jack Scott; Peter Sykes; Stephen Spencer; Carol Stallings; Roy Stonehouse; Derek Ware; Brian Wenham; Richard Williams; Colin Willock: and my wife, Vivien, son Nicholas, and daughter Rebecca for their patience and good judgement.

The publishers would like to thank the following people for supplying the photographs in this book:

All-sport 35 (centre)
Anglia TV 16 (right)
BBC Enterprises 8, 26, 27
BBC Photographs 2 (Sue Lawley), 10, 16 (bottom left), 34 (top), 35 (bottom), 36 (top), 39, 46 (bottom), 48 (top), 50 (bottom left), 72, 74 (top right), 78 (top and bottom left), 79 (top right), 84 (left)
Bird's Eye Wall's 24 (bottom)
Blue Peter 68, 69
British Telecom/Dorland Advertising 25 (centre)
Brooke Bond Oxo 24 (top right)
Cadbury-Schweppes/Boase Massimi Pollit 60 (bottom)
Camera Press 78 (top and bottom right), 79 (top and bottom left, top and bottom centre)
Central Independent Television 16 (top left)

Centre for Remote Sensing 84 (top right)
Channel 4 Television 2 (The Tube, No Problem, Wood & Walters, Steve Davis, Everybody Here), 3 (Sleeping Beauty, American Football), 38, 57 (top, centre and bottom right), 74 (top and bottom left, bottom right), 85 (left)
Coca Cola/McCann-Erickson 25 (bottom)
Bruce Coleman/G.D. Plage 2 (tiger)
Peter Day 28 (top left and right, bottom left)
Peter Dunne 75
Allan Grainger 7, 9, 28 (bottom right), 29, 61, 62 (top), 63 (top left and right), 80, 82, 83 (left)
Granada Television 12, 13, 18 (centre and bottom left), 19 (top and bottom tight), 70 (top)
Ray Hodges Associates 47 (bottom right)
ICI/Welbeck Public Relations 24 (top left)
ITN 4 (inset), 79 (bottom right), 81, 83 (right)
Alf Joint 59 (bottom)
Rob Judges 50 (centre right)
London Weekend Television 3 (Lenny Henry), 6 (top left and bottom right)
Meteorological Office 84 (bottom right), 85 (right)
Midland Bank 60 (centre)
MPL/Richard Monkton 47 (bottom left)
National Film Archive 56, 57 (top and bottom left)
Oracle 51 (bottom)
Open University 54, 55
Duncan Paul 6 (bottom left)
Qantas 25 (top)
Radio Times 66, 67
RHM Foods/Collett Dickinson Pearce 60 (top)
Scope Features 6 (top right), 46 (top), 47 (top left, top and centre right), 48 (bottom), 49
Warren Shaffer 11, 18 (top left and

right), 19 (bottom left), 20, 21, 86
Survival Anglia 52, 53
Jeffrey Tabberner 42, 43 (all)
Thames Television 3 (Minder), 4–5 (top), 34 (centre and bottom), 35 (top), 36 (bottom), 37, 40, 41, 50 (top right, centre left and bottom right), 51 (top), 59, 70 (bottom), 71, 76, 77
Tomorrow's World 30, 31
TVTimes 67
Tyne Tees Television 85 (bottom right)
Richard Williams Animation (Shell UK/Ogilvy and Mather), 62 (centre) (Cadbury-Schweppes/Boase Massimi Pollit) 62 (bottom), (Sterling Health/Benton and Bowles) 63 (bottom), (Watney Mann Truman) 63 (centre)

The illustrations are by:

Ed Carr
Bob Chapman
Mike Gornall
David Murray
Jon Riley

Front cover photographs:
  Rob Judges
  Rex Features
Photograph of author:
  Jeffrey Tabberner

To Viv

Oxford University Press, Walton Street, Oxford OX2 6DP

Oxford New York Toronto
Delhi Bombay Calcutta Madras Karachi
Petaling Jaya Singapore Hong Kong Tokyo
Nairobi Dar es Salaam Cape Town
Melbourne Auckland

and associated companies in
Beirut Berlin Ibadan Nicosia

Oxford is a trade mark of Oxford University Press

British Library Cataloguing in Publication Data

Kelly, Chris
The telebook.
1. Television—Juvenile literature
I. Title
621.388   TK6640

ISBN 0-19-273156-3

Set by Tradespools Ltd., Frome, Somerset
Printed in Hong Kong